When Parents Ask for Help

Everyday Issues through an Asset-Building Lens

Handouts for People Raising Adolescents / *By Renie Howard*

When Parents Ask for Help: Everyday Issues through an Asset-Building Lens
Renie Howard
Search Institute® and Development Assets® are trademarks of Search Institute.
Copyright © 2003 by Search Institute

Printed on recycled paper in the United States of America.

Search Institute, 615 First Avenue NE, Suite 125, Minneapolis, MN 55413
612-376-8955; 800-888-7828; www.search-institute.org

Editors: Jennifer Griffin-Wiesner, Rebecca Aldridge
Design/Typesetting: Sheila Chin Morris
Production: Mary Ellen Buscher

Library of Congress Cataloging-in-Publication Data
Howard, Renie, 1955-
    When parents ask for help: everyday issues through an asset-building
lens: handouts for people raising adolescents / Renie Howard.
        p. cm.
    ISBN 1-57482-429-5 (alk. paper)
1. Parent and teenager. 2. Teenagers--Family relationships. 3. Adolescence. I. Title.
HQ799.15.H69 2003
649'.125--dc21

                                              2003005526

About Search Institute

Search Institute is an independent, nonprofit, nonsectarian organization whose mission is to provide leadership, knowledge, and resources to promote healthy children, youth, and communities. The institute collaborates with others to promote long-term organizational and cultural change that supports its mission. For a free information packet, call 800-888-7828.

Search Institute's Healthy Communities • Healthy Youth initiative seeks to unite individuals, organizations, and their leaders to join together in nurturing competent, caring, and responsible children and adolescents. The founding national sponsor for Healthy Communities • Healthy Youth is Thrivent Financial for Lutherans, a not-for-profit fraternal benefit society providing financial services and community service opportunities for Lutherans nationwide.

About This Resource

Funding for *When Parents Ask for Help: Everyday Issues through an Asset-Building Lens* was provided by the Donald W. Reynolds Foundation, a national philanthropic organization founded in 1954 by the late media entrepreneur for whom it is named. Reynolds was the founder and principal owner of the Donrey Media Group. Headquartered in Las Vegas, it is one of the largest private foundations in the United States.

For Matthew
With love and gratitude
And for Noah and Sarah

When Parents Ask for Help:

Everyday Issues through an Asset-Building Lens

TABLE OF CONTENTS / Continued

Introduction for Parenting Professionals

The aim of this publication is to provide professionals communicating or working with parents or other caregivers the tools to help them face the challenges of raising an adolescent. Our intent is to help parents meet these challenges with creativity, humor, compassion for themselves and their adolescent children, and a deep appreciation of their children's unique gifts and abilities. The developmental asset approach gives families and communities indispensable tools for creating a rich and caring environment in which young people—and their parents—can find the support they need to learn, grow, and flourish.

HOW TO USE THIS BOOK

This book is designed for use by anyone who is helping caregivers meet the challenges of raising adolescent children, whether a parent educator, family mediator, school counselor, etc. Each article can be reproduced for use as a handout, newsletter, or other resource that is distributed to parents or guardians. You may want to pass the articles out at weekly parenting groups, starting with the introduction for parents and other caregivers and then distributing the articles, issue by issue, as appropriate. These articles make good handouts for parent support groups as well. Or, consider making copies of several of the articles and place them in a high-traffic area with other free resources.

You can also use these articles on a more individual basis. Imagine a distraught stepfather comes to you about the fights he has been having with his 14-year-old stepdaughter. Their arguments revolve around her dating an older guy and missing curfew. In this case, you may want to give the stepfather the handouts on curfew, together with those on dating, getting along: parents and adolescents, and sexuality. And for any parent new to the 40 developmental assets, always include the article "Introduction for Parents or Other Caregivers." In the wake of a tragic event, at any community meeting, articles on themes such as tragedy, school violence, and race and ethnicity may be good resources to pass out.

Each handout offers practical suggestions for dealing with a common parenting issue through the lens of the asset-building model. The subheads in each chapter correspond to specific assets or asset categories that are relevant to the matter at hand. You can use the handout on page 3 of this section to help parents target what areas they would like help with in their own families.

These articles provide a starting place for caregivers. Once parents or guardians have had a chance to absorb a handout's information and want to go further, recommend something appropriate from the list of books and resources with which you're familiar.

OFFERING HOPE

"It's the toughest job you'll ever love." This Peace Corps slogan could be written into the job description for parenting. Nothing can truly prepare a parent or guardian for all the day-to-day challenges of raising a family. And raising an adolescent can be especially challenging; it's a time of rapid change, when a young person is busy trying to discover who he or she is. Suddenly, the role a parent has played for years may seem less clear, and he or she may not know what to do.

So what action can you take when the caregivers of adolescents come to you for help? What can you offer that will really make a difference? You know these guardians are probably tired and stressed out, and almost certainly they are feeling some combination of frustration and insecurity—maybe even desperation—about their children's shortcomings, their own, or both. They're counting on you to see what they need and help them get it.

First of all, they need reassurance. They need to know they're not crazy, that their children aren't deviant, that other families experience similar difficulties. And then these caregivers need to know there's something they can do, action they can take, a new way to look at things. They need sound, practical ideas that work. They need to know there is hope.

The handout articles in this book are designed to offer both reassurance and hope. Each one addresses a specific dilemma common to parents of adolescents. Rather than viewing a dilemma as an obstacle, the developmental assets concept is offered as a way to think differently. The articles provide practical steps for helping parents deal with each situation in constructive ways that contribute to a greater sense of well-being for all concerned.

WHAT ARE DEVELOPMENTAL ASSETS?

Developmental assets are positive experiences and qualities that all people, not just caregivers, have the power to bring into the lives of youth. These social and emotional resources spread across eight broad areas of human development and therefore provide young people with a sense of security. Research by Search Institute shows that the more developmental assets a young person has, the better equipped he or she is to make wise choices, handle the pressures of daily living, and find meaning and fulfillment in life. (A complete list of the assets appears on pages 2–3 and 4–5 [Spanish] of the next section.)

The asset model comes from Search Institute in Minneapolis, Minnesota, a nonprofit agency that conducts research on children and youth. At Search Institute, much reading, thinking, and discussion took place about what young people need to succeed. Developmental assets identify the key resources, advantages, and qualities young people need to mature into caring, responsible, and happy adults. Once the list of 40 developmental assets was in place, researchers looked for and found hundreds of studies that supported the choice of these assets.

Researchers also designed a survey to measure the number of assets that 6th- through 12th-grade students in hundreds of different communities were experiencing in their everyday lives. They found that the more assets young people have, the better equipped they are to make wise choices, handle the pressures of daily living, and find meaning and fulfillment in life. If you are unfamiliar with the developmental assets, visit the Search Institute Web site at www.search-institute.org. There you'll find information on a number of helpful resources, including *Developmental Assets: A Synthesis of the Scientific Research on Adolescent Development* by Peter C. Scales and Nancy Leffert.

ASSETS FOR PARENTS

Although the asset model focuses on young people, clearly there are key resources, advantages, and qualities that parents need in order to succeed as well. Adequate support, self-care, and personal growth for parents are consistent themes throughout these articles.

Just as asset building fosters a sense of connection between young people and caring adults, it also encourages parents to strengthen their own connections within their communities. The more "plugged-in" parents are to sources of support—friends, family, neighbors, schools, places of worship—the better prepared they will be to meet the ongoing and new challenges of parenting.

Similarly, guardians who have their own needs met will be better equipped to care for their children with energy and imagination. Taking time for themselves, knowing when they need a break, and being able to ask for help are not only important parenting skills but also skills necessary for any adult.

Parents also need to be open to learning and growing in their own lives. Parenting is a transformational experience; we are changed by it. Our children teach us as surely as we teach them. Many of the issues discussed in this book require parents to examine their own attitudes and beliefs on a given topic, so that they can more effectively help their children explore and learn.

Family Topics Checklist

Our family could use some guidance or new ideas about the following topics:

Home and Family
_____ Getting along: Parents and adolescents (arguing, conflict, differences)
_____ Getting along: Brothers and sisters (fighting, blaming, and finger-pointing)
_____ TV (setting limits, creating options)
_____ The Internet (setting limits, making surfing safe)
_____ Chores (responsibilities, getting them done)
_____ Curfew (rules, knowing where your children are)
_____ Food (eating healthfully, eating together)

School
_____ School and homework (struggling, boredom, planning)
_____ Graduation and beyond (the future, life after high school)
_____ Bullying/Being Bullied (picking on others, being a victim)
_____ School violence (weapons, shootings)

Companions
_____ Friends (good ones, bad ones)
_____ Other caring, responsible adults (relatives, friends, mentors)
_____ Dating (hanging out, dates, partners)
_____ Sexuality (touching, kissing, having sex)

Emotions
_____ Stress management (regaining power, regaining control)
_____ Self-acceptance (liking ourselves)
_____ Anger management (finding peace, calming down)
_____ Depression (feeling intense sadness, feeling alone)

Work
_____ Jobs outside the home (work and other responsibilities)
_____ Money (spending, saving, giving)

Image
_____ Appearance (piercing, tattoos, unconventional clothes)
_____ Body image (feeling fat, feeling ugly)

The Caregiver
_____ Separation/Divorce (caring for yourself and your children)
_____ Single parenting (taking care of *your* needs)

Special Issues
_____ Race and ethnicity (awareness, discrimination, equality)
_____ Substance abuse (alcohol, other drugs)
_____ Tragedy (suicides, terrorist attacks, accidents)

Introduction for Parents or Other Caregivers

Raising children has been compared to riding a roller coaster—thrilling, terrifying, and full of ups and downs. Most parents and other caregivers probably wouldn't argue with that assessment. And most parents would probably agree that the ride gets *really* interesting during their children's adolescent years.

Some bumps and unexpected turns are bound to occur, but the ride doesn't have to be a sheer vertical drop. You can do a lot to make your children's transition from childhood to adulthood a more serene, often enjoyable, passage for your family. And it may be comforting to know that you are certainly not the only family on the ride.

DEVELOPMENTAL ASSETS

The developmental asset model is an approach designed to help identify the key resources, advantages, and qualities young people need to mature into caring, responsible, and happy adults. These social and emotional resources provide a sense of security. The more assets a young person has, the better equipped he or she is to make wise choices, handle the pressures of daily living, and find meaning and fulfillment in life. (A complete list of the assets appears on pages 2–3 and 4–5 [Spanish] of this handout.)

ASSETS FOR PARENTS

Although the asset model focuses on young people, clearly there are key resources, advantages, and qualities that parents need in order to succeed as well. Adequate support, self-care, and personal growth for caregivers are consistent themes throughout these articles.

Just as asset building fosters a sense of connection between young people and caring adults, it also encourages parents to strengthen their own connections within their communities. The more connected you are to sources of support—friends, family, neighbors, schools, places of worship—the better prepared you will be to meet the challenges of parenting.

Similarly, guardians who are able to meet their own needs will be better equipped to care for their children with energy and imagination. Taking time for yourself, knowing when you need a break, and being able to ask for help are not only important parenting skills but also skills necessary for any adult.

Parents also need to be open to learning and growing in

their own lives. Parenting is a transformational experience; we are changed by it. Our children teach us as surely as we teach them. Many of the issues discussed in this book ask you to examine your own attitudes and beliefs on a given topic so that you can more effectively help your children explore and learn.

THE ASSET MODEL

The asset model comes from Search Institute in Minneapolis, Minnesota, a nonprofit organization that conducts research on children and youth. At Search Institute, much reading, thinking, and discussion took place about what young people need to succeed. Once the list of 40 developmental assets was in place, researchers looked for and found hundreds of studies that supported the choice of these assets.

Researchers also designed a survey to measure the number of assets that 6th- through 12th-grade students in hundreds of different communities were experiencing in their everyday lives. They found that the more assets young people have, the better off they seemed to be—the overall theme being that young people need to feel a strong sense of connection to caring adults.

The 40 assets are evenly divided into two broad categories, external assets and internal assets. These subcategories are further broken down into smaller groups, each of which is identified by a key concept, such as "Support," or "Social Competencies." The list on the next page identifies the 20 external assets and the 20 internal assets, and it places each within its key concept group.

MAINTAINING EQUILIBRIUM

An asset-building approach to raising an adolescent can help you identify the areas in which your child has plenty of resources and those in which more support or focus would be helpful. The more assets young people have, the better they are able to keep their balance when life throws in some surprising twists and turns (which it certainly has a way of doing). And knowing your child has the internal and external resources to cope with life's ups and downs makes it more likely that you can relax and enjoy the ride.

40 Developmental Assets

EXTERNAL ASSETS

SUPPORT (Assets 1–6)

Family Support—Family life provides high levels of love and support.

Positive Family Communication—Young person and her or his parent(s) communicate positively, and young person is willing to seek advice and counsel from parent(s).

Other Adult Relationships—Young person receives support from three or more nonparent adults.

Caring Neighborhood—Young person experiences caring neighbors.

Caring School Climate—School provides a caring, encouraging environment.

Parent Involvement in Schooling—Parent(s) are actively involved in helping young person succeed in school.

EMPOWERMENT (Assets 7–10)

Community Values Youth—Young person perceives that adults in the community value youth.

Youth as Resources—Young people are given useful roles in the community.

Service to Others—Young person serves in the community one hour or more per week.

Safety—Young person feels safe at home, at school, and in the neighborhood.

BOUNDARIES AND EXPECTATIONS (Assets 11–16)

Family Boundaries—Family has clear rules and consequences and monitors the young person's whereabouts.

School Boundaries—School provides clear rules and consequences.

Neighborhood Boundaries—Neighbors take responsibility for monitoring young people's behavior.

Adult Role Models—Parent(s) and other adults model positive, responsible behavior.

Positive Peer Influence—Young person's best friends model responsible behavior.

High Expectations—Both parent(s) and teachers encourage the young person to do well.

CONSTRUCTIVE USE OF TIME (Assets 17–20)

Creative Activities—Young person spends three or more hours per week in lessons or practice in music, theater, or other arts.

Youth Programs—Young person spends three or more hours per week in sports, clubs, or organizations at school and/or in the community.

Religious Community—Young person spends one or more hours per week in activities in a religious institution.

Time at Home—Young person is out with friends "with nothing special to do" two or fewer nights per week.

INTERNAL ASSETS

COMMITMENT TO LEARNING (Assets 21–25)

Achievement Motivation—Young person is motivated to do well in school.

School Engagement—Young person is actively engaged in learning.

Homework—Young person reports doing at least one hour of homework every school day.

Bonding to School—Young person cares about her or his school.

Reading for Pleasure—Young person reads for pleasure three or more hours per week.

POSITIVE VALUES (Assets 26–31)

Caring—Young person places high value on helping other people.

Equality and Social Justice—Young person places high value on promoting equality and reducing hunger and poverty.

Integrity—Young person acts on convictions and stands up for her or his beliefs.

Honesty—Young person "tells the truth even when it is not easy."

Responsibility—Young person accepts and takes personal responsibility.

Restraint—Young person believes it is important not to be sexually active or to use alcohol or other drugs.

SOCIAL COMPETENCIES (Assets 32–36)

Planning and Decision Making—Young person knows how to plan ahead and make choices.

Interpersonal Competence—Young person has empathy, sensitivity, and friendship skills.

Cultural Competence—Young person has knowledge of and comfort with people of different cultural/racial/ethnic backgrounds.

Resistance Skills—Young person can resist negative peer pressure and dangerous situations.

Peaceful Conflict Resolution—Young person seeks to resolve conflict nonviolently.

POSITIVE IDENTITY (Assets 37–40)

Personal Power—Young person feels he or she has control over "things that happen to me."

Self-Esteem—Young person reports having a high self-esteem.

Sense of Purpose—Young person reports that "my life has a purpose."

Positive View of Personal Future—Young person is optimistic about her or his personal future.

40 Elementos Fundamentales Del Desarrollo

La investigación realizada por el Instituto Search ha identificado los siguientes elementos fundamentales del desarrollo como instrumentos para ayudar a los jóvenes a crecer sanos, interesados en el bienestar común y a ser responsables.

ELEMENTOS FUNDAMENTALES EXTERNOS

APOYO

Apoyo familiar—La vida familiar brinda altos niveles de amor y apoyo.

Comunicación familiar positiva—El (La) joven y sus padres se comunican positivamente. Los jóvenes están dispuestos a buscar consejo y consuelo en sus padres.

Otras relaciones con adultos—Además de sus padres, los jóvenes reciben apoyo de tres o más personas adultas que no son sus parientes.

Una comunidad comprometida—El (La) joven experimenta el interés de sus vecinos por su bienestar.

Un plantel educativo que se interesa por el (la) joven—La escuela proporciona un ambiente que anima y se preocupa por la juventud.

La participación de los padres en las actividades escolares—Los padres participan activamente ayudando a los jóvenes a tener éxito en la escuela.

FORTALECIMIENTO

La comunidad valora a la juventud—El (La) joven percibe que los adultos en la comunidad valoran a la juventud.

La juventud como un recurso—Se le brinda a los jóvenes la oportunidad de tomar un papel útil en la comunidad.

Servicio a los demás—La gente joven participa brindando servicios a su comunidad una hora o más a la semana.

Seguridad—Los jóvenes se sienten seguros en casa, en la escuela y en el vecindario.

LÍMITES Y EXPECTATIVAS

Límites familiares—La familia tiene reglas y consecuencias bien claras, además vigila las actividades de los jóvenes.

Límites escolares—En la escuela proporciona reglas y consecuencias bien claras.

Límites vecinales—Los vecinos asumen la responsabilidad de vigilar el comportamiento de los jóvenes.

El comportamiento de los adultos como ejemplo—Los padres y otros adultos tienen un comportamiento positivo y responsable.

Compañeros como influencia positiva—Los mejores amigos del (la) joven son un buen ejemplo de comportamiento responsable.

Altas expectativas—Ambos padres y maestros motivan a los jóvenes para que tengan éxito.

USO CONSTRUCTIVO DEL TIEMPO

Actividades creativas—Los jóvenes pasan tres horas o más a la semana en lecciones de música, teatro u otras artes.

Programas juveniles—Los jóvenes pasan tres horas o más a la semana practicando algún deporte, o en organizaciones en la escuela o de la comunidad.

Comunidad religiosa—Los jóvenes pasan una hora o más a la semana en actividades organizadas por alguna institución religiosa.

Tiempo en casa—Los jóvenes conviven con sus amigos "sin nada especial que hacer" dos o pocas noches por semana.

ELEMENTOS FUNDAMENTALES INTERNOS

COMPROMISO CON EL APRENDIZAJE

Motivación por sus logros—El (La) joven es motivado(a) para que salga bien en la escuela.

Compromiso con la escuela—El (La) joven participa activamente con el aprendizaje.

Tarea—El (La) joven debe hacer su tarea escolar por lo menos durante una hora cada día de clases.

Preocuparse por la escuela—Al (A la) joven debe importarle su escuela.

Leer por placer—El (La) joven lee por placer tres horas o más por semana.

VALORES POSITIVOS

Preocuparse por los demás—El (La) joven valora ayudar a los demás.

Igualdad y justicia social—Para el (la) joven tiene mucho valor el promover la igualdad y reducir el hambre y la pobreza.

Integridad—El (La) joven actúa con convicción y defiende sus creencias.

Honestidad—El (La) joven "dice la verdad aún cuando esto no sea fácil".

Responsabilidad—El (La) joven acepta y toma responsabilidad por su persona.

Abstinencia—El (La) joven cree que es importante no estar activo(a) sexualmente, ni usar alcohol u otras drogas.

CAPACIDAD SOCIAL

Planeación y toma de decisiones—El (La) joven sabe cómo planear y hacer elecciones.

Capacidad interpersonal—El (La) joven es sympático, sensible y hábil para hacer amistades.

Capacidad cultural—El (La) joven tiene conocimiento de y sabe convivir con gente de diferente marco cultural, racial o étnico.

Habilidad de resistencia—El (La) joven puede resistir la presión negativa de los compañeros así como las situaciones peligrosas.

Solución pacífica de conflictos—El (La) joven busca resolver los conflictos sin violencia.

IDENTIDAD POSITIVA

Poder personal—El (La) joven siente que él o ella tiene el control de "las cosas que le suceden".

Auto-estima—El (La) joven afirma tener una alta auto-estima.

Sentido de propósito—El (La) joven afirma que "mi vida tiene un propósito".

Visión positiva del futuro personal—El (La) joven es optimista sobre su futuro mismo.

Parents' Developmental Assets Daily Checklist

You can use the assets to help you choose the ways you want to intentionally build the strengths of your child. Try using this checklist as a start or create your own.

Today I will

☐ ask how my child is doing. (Asset #2)

☐ really listen to my child. (Asset #33)

☐ act responsibly. (Asset #30)

☐ be honest with my spouse, kids, friends, neighbors—even salespeople. (Asset #29)

☐ offer my child opportunities to contribute to the family and to others. (Assets #7, 8, 9)

☐ notice what's happening in my neighborhood. (Asset #13)

☐ ask what my child learned, liked, and didn't like in school. (Asset #6)

☐ tell my child about my day. (Asset #2)

☐ keep track of what my child is doing. (Asset #11)

☐ provide a quiet place for homework. (Asset #23)

☐ know when to turn off the TV. (Asset #20)

☐ give my child ways to grow in body, mind, and spirit. (Assets #17, 18, 19)

☐ tell my child one thing I love or appreciate about her or him. (Asset #38)

Getting Along: Parents and Adolescents

Your Dilemma:

**"Sometimes I think Selena believes I was put here to be at her beck and call.
I need to make her understand how busy my schedule is, too."**
or
"Every time Josh and I talk, he winds up yelling and slamming the door!"

ACTION TIPS

◆ Learn about techniques for resolving conflict peacefully, and teach them to your family. Ask your school's guidance counselor or a professional counselor to recommend reading materials on this topic, or see if workshops or seminars are available in your community.

◆ Show affection and verbally support your children as much as possible.

◆ Spend time together as a family.

◆ Make positive communication a priority. Seek out opportunities to talk with your children. Listen to what they have to say.

◆ Set some ground rules for expressing strong emotions. For example, you might agree that it's okay to say you're angry, but not to call each other names. Be sure everyone abides by these rules.

◆ Be clear about what you expect from your children with regard to school, friends, chores and obligations, and how they behave at home. Expect their best from them, but give them room to make mistakes.

◆ Celebrate their unique gifts and their successes. Let them know what you appreciate about them.

FACT: Forty-five percent of youth say they know how
to resolve conflicts peacefully.

From: *Developmental Assets: A Profile of Your Youth,* Executive Summary for Search Institute

Most of us have moments or even days when we wish we could resign from parenting or at least take an extra-long break. The job's just too relentless, too thankless, too hard. We ask ourselves: What happened to the sweet child who used to love spending time with me? Who is this moody person who sometimes seems to resent my very existence but still wants a ride to Rachel's party? Why is it so hard to get along?

We can do much to make things more peaceful where we live. We can't control our children's behavior, but we can control our own. We can learn peaceful ways to resolve conflicts. And we can help create a supportive and positive environment in which everyone will be more inclined to get along.

The developmental assets are positive qualities, experiences, and skills that children need to grow up healthy and responsible. Parents, grandparents, stepparents, or any other guardian of a child can use these assets as a framework to help them think through the new experiences they're encountering with their children. When dealing with the issue of living together in harmony, the assets you may want to consider looking at for guidance are Peaceful Conflict Resolution, Family Support, Positive Family Communication, Family Boundaries, Other Adult Relationships, High Expectations, and Self-Esteem.

ASSET TYPE	ASSET NAME	ASSET DESCRIPTION
Social Competencies	Peaceful Conflict Resolution	Young people seek to resolve conflicts nonviolently.
Support	Family Support	Young people feel loved and supported in their family.
Support	Positive Family Communication	Young people turn to their parents for advice and support. They have frequent, in-depth conversations with each other on a variety of topics. Parents are approachable and available when their children want to talk.
Boundaries and Expectations	Family Boundaries	Parents set clear rules and consequences for their children's behavior. They monitor their children's whereabouts.
Support	Other Adult Relationships	Young people know other adults besides their parents they can turn to for advice and support. They have frequent, in-depth conversations with them. Ideally, three or more adults play this role in their lives.
Boundaries and Expectations	High Expectations	Parents and teachers encourage young people to do well.
Positive Identity	Self-Esteem	Young people feel good about themselves.

PEACEFUL CONFLICT RESOLUTION

Resolving conflict peacefully is an important skill for young people and one we can play a key role in teaching them. Approaching conflict as an opportunity for learning about each other is one way to create more space for resolution. **When conflicts arise, take the time to listen to each other.** If a particular topic is sensitive, or if the discussion has become especially heated, you may want to take some time apart before continuing. There are many techniques for conflict resolution; your school's guidance counselor or librarian may be able to recommend some books on the subject that you could read as a family.

One simple and effective technique is called "mirroring." This involves reflecting back the other person's point of view. One person speaks first (you can flip a coin if necessary), and the other listens carefully and attentively, without interrupting (or making faces or showing signs of boredom or impatience). When the speaker is finished, the listener repeats (mirrors) what the speaker said with as much clarity and detail as possible. The speaker then adds or clarifies anything that the listener missed or misunderstood. Then the listener makes two comments or statements. The first statement validates what the speaker expressed. (For example, "I hear you saying that you had a hard day.") Then the listener makes an empathetic statement (For example, "If I were you, I would feel sad/confused/angry, etc.") Then—and this is the crucial part—both parties wait 24 hours before switching roles. (The time period might be modified for less volatile issues.)

The waiting period gives the speaker the opportunity to feel fully heard, without having to defend against a rebuttal. And it gives the listener the opportunity to absorb what was said, without quickly jumping back into her or his own position. When used properly, mirroring can be a powerful tool for gaining insight into another person's perspective.

FAMILY SUPPORT

In the frenzy of everyday life, it's easy to lose sight of some of the simple things that can help create a more supportive and peaceful environment in your home. Going the extra mile may seem an impossible distance at times, but the benefits can be immediate and far-reaching. For example, **make a special effort to show your love for your adolescent children—without expecting anything in return.** Pay attention to your body language, and let it express your care and concern. Be physically affectionate and verbally supportive. Remember to praise your children for the things they're doing well, and tell them you love them—don't assume they know.

Spend time together as a family. Try to have at least one meal together every day, if possible, or at least a few times a week, and take the opportunity to enjoy each other's company. Have a family game or music night once a week. If possible, spend time with each child individually. Schedule an hour or two each week (or at least once a month) for each child, and make it a special time. Do something fun and interesting together, and make it clear that this time is important to you.

POSITIVE FAMILY COMMUNICATION

Make communication a priority in your family. **Let your children know that you're always available to talk.** The time you invest in positive communication will be more than recovered in peace and calm. When your children come to you with a question, give them your full attention—set down your book or turn away from the computer. If you're busy with something important, tell them when you'll be finished and then follow up by seeking them out.

And **when they talk, really listen.** Try to hear what they're saying without judgment or criticism. Simply acknowledging their position before you respond can go a long way toward creating greater trust and understanding. Listen for the piece you both have in common and work from there. Giving them your full attention will also help keep discussions focused on the issue at hand, rather than degenerating into argument and accusation. Avoid the temptation to interrupt or correct them. Help them develop a "feelings vocabulary" so they know how to express emotions in a direct and constructive way.

Ask your children's opinions on important matters— everything from what color to paint the kitchen to what's going on in the Middle East and other parts of the world. Take turns choosing topics for family discussions. And let them know their opinions are valid and important. You don't have to agree with them. But it's important to provide a safe place for them to discuss their ideas and develop their critical thinking skills.

As much as possible, **avoid making certain topics off limits.** You're entitled to your privacy, of course, and so are your children. But let them know you'll do your best to answer sincere and respectful questions, and to hear what they have to say on virtually any subject. If you're uncomfortable with some topics, get help to learn how to approach them. For example, the guidance counselor at your school or your family clinic may have information about how to talk to young people about sexuality, HIV/AIDS, substance abuse, and other tough topics.

Recognize the importance of respect to many young people. Talk with your children about what this means to each of you and agree to some basic ground rules for showing respect in your family.

FAMILY BOUNDARIES

 If discussions have a tendency to explode in your family, **set some ground rules that everyone can uphold.** For example, you might establish a rule that expressing anger is okay (as in "I feel really angry when you do that"), but yelling and calling people names are not. Be sure you abide by these rules.

Recognize when you need a time out. If a discussion has escalated into an argument and you can't seem to step back from your position, take a break. Put the conversation on hold by telling your child you need a break, and leave the room (or the house if necessary). Call a friend, go for a walk, write in your journal. Pick up the discussion again when you feel able to bring some clarity and restraint to it.

Remember that humor can be a great ally, when used respectfully. **Try to see the humor in the situation, and find ways to lighten up your view of yourself and your children.** Sharing a laugh together can be a great way to remember what you like about each other.

Keep a calendar with everyone's schedule clearly noted on it. Knowing where everyone is expected to be at a given time will help reduce misunderstandings and make home life run more smoothly.

OTHER ADULT RELATIONSHIPS

 Having other caring adults in their lives helps young people gain perspective on their life at home and gives them a place to blow off steam when things get difficult. It also helps them form nurturing relationships with role models who may be able to shed some light on getting along with their folks.

Take stock of the relationships your child has with other trusted adults. Are there relatives, neighbors, or friends who regularly spend time with your child? Or are there adults who might be interested in getting involved in this way if you ask them? See if your school offers a mentoring program. Or talk to the youth director in your place of worship to see if there might be an adult in the congregation who has interests in common with your child. Get to know these people yourself to be sure you're comfortable with the relationship. You might invite them to dinner, for example, as a way for the family to get to know them.

HIGH EXPECTATIONS

 Let your children know that all close relationships have bumpy moments. Tell them you expect disagreement at times, but you also expect every-

one to make an effort to work through conflict in agreed-upon ways.

Be clear about what you expect from your children. Tell them what your expectations are with regard to school, friends, chores, and their relationship with you and why you expect these things. Ask them what they expect from themselves and whether they consider your expectations fair. Ask what their expectations are of you as a caregiver. Revisit these questions from time to time and make sure you're in agreement about what's expected.

Hold them accountable for their actions, but allow them room to make mistakes and realize their limits. For example, if you know your child can get high grades, and he or she brings home a low grade in science, talk about the situation. Be direct but not confrontational. Ask what happened and what kind of help he or she needs. Is peer tutoring available? Talk to the science teacher and guidance counselor about getting additional help. And if your child has a learning disability, it may not be reasonable to expect high marks in all subjects in the first place.

Above all, **applaud your children's accomplishments.** Notice when they're fulfilling or exceeding your expectations, even in small ways. If your child has been taking out the garbage without being reminded, acknowledge what a pleasure it is not to have to worry about that.

SELF-ESTEEM

Young people who feel good about themselves are less likely to act out in destructive ways. **Actively seek out ways to affirm your children's self-worth.** Show interest in their activities, tell them specific qualities you appreciate in them, celebrate their unique gifts and their successes, and get to know their friends. Surprise them occasionally with a small gift for no reason. Or learn about something they're interested in, and share what you've discovered. Plan a "field trip" somewhere of interest to them. Participate in their school and other activities. And when they make mistakes, make a point of distinguishing between the behavior and the child.

KEEPING THE PEACE

Getting along with adolescents can be challenging at times, no doubt about it. Of course, they probably feel the same way about us! The skills we teach them now for getting along with other members of their family will serve them well in everything they do.

WAYS TO SHOW YOU'RE THERE, WAYS TO SHOW YOU CARE

◆ Be affectionate. Give hugs as often as possible, but respect your children's personal "space."

◆ Look your children in the eye when talking to them. Give them your undivided attention.

◆ Use loving words daily. Say things like: "I care about you." "I think you're great." "You're terrific."

◆ Act lovingly toward yourself. Modeling affection goes a long way.

30 HELPFUL HINTS FOR GETTING ALONG AS A FAMILY

Do . . .

Say "Please" and "Thank you."

Use proper table manners.

Disagree without being disagreeable.

Ask without yelling.

Listen attentively.

Be willing to compromise.

Treat others as you would like to be treated.

Share willingly.

Treat each other's property with care and respect.

Apologize sincerely when apologies are called for.

Celebrate each other's successes.

Try to understand each other's pain.

Be thoughtful of each other—especially if you know a family member is having a difficult day.

Take responsibility for your own actions and words.

Smile.

Do not . . .

Lie.

Hit.

Snoop.

Whine.

Interrupt.

Use crude language.

Take each other's belongings without asking.

Tell each other's secrets.

Ignore each other's requests.

Be afraid to speak up when you feel something is wrong.

Spend all day or night on the telephone.

Embarrass your parents, siblings, or children in front of their friends.

Make plans for each other without making sure they're okay in advance.

Forget to do your chores.

Treat each other rudely.

Getting Along: Brothers and Sisters

Your Dilemma:

**"Dan and Deanna are at it constantly.
The fighting and yelling—it's driving us crazy."**
or
**"Leticia's jealous and constantly arguing with Melissa
because Melissa is in gymnastics and we spend
a lot of time going to her meets."**

ACTION TIPS

◆ When bickering starts, acknowledge both parties' emotions. Encourage your children to express their feelings clearly and respectfully, and give your full attention to what they say.

◆ Encourage your children to spend time together, doing things they both enjoy.

◆ Set ground rules about what is okay and what's not okay.

◆ Avoid taking sides when brothers and sisters argue.

◆ Allow siblings to resolve most conflicts on their own, but get involved when the situation threatens to become emotionally or physically hurtful.

◆ Appreciate your children for the individuals they are. Spend time with each of them alone and show interest in their talents and pursuits.

FACT: In one survey, job demands and bickering among their children were the top items that caregivers said made parenting harder.

From: *Building Strong Families,* YMCA and Search Institute

For many children, their first experience in learning how to get along with other people comes from living with their brothers and sisters. But no matter how well-behaved the kids, when you have at least two in the house, there are bound to be arguments. Some brothers and sisters, however, may have more issues than others. As parents, we want peace, but that may simply not be possible. When should we dive in, and when should we let them work it out themselves? How can we help make peace in our family?

The developmental assets are positive qualities, experiences, and skills that children need to grow up healthy and responsible. Parents, grandparents, stepparents, or any other guardian of a child can use these assets as a framework to help them think through the new experiences they're encountering with their children. When dealing with issues of sibling rivalry in your family, the assets you may want to consider looking at for guidance are Positive Family Communication, Family Boundaries, Peaceful Conflict Resolution, Family Support, and Interpersonal Competence.

ASSET TYPE	ASSET NAME	ASSET DESCRIPTION
Support	Positive Family Communication	Young people turn to their parents for advice and support. They have frequent, in-depth conversations with each other on a variety of topics. Parents are approachable and available when their children want to talk.
Boundaries and Expectations	Family Boundaries	Parents set clear rules and consequences for their children's behavior. They monitor their children's whereabouts.
Social Competencies	Peaceful Conflict Resolution	Young people seek to resolve conflicts nonviolently.
Support	Family Support	Young people feel loved and supported in their family.
Social Competencies	Interpersonal Competence	Young people have empathy, sensitivity, and friendship skills.

POSITIVE FAMILY COMMUNICATION

Parents and guardians can **begin to deal with sibling rivalry by telling their children that disagreements are normal but that constant fighting is upsetting** and you value a peaceful home.

Blaming and finger-pointing often accompany an argument. Sometimes caregivers have the inclination to stop the bickering and say something such as, "Don't complain. She's your only sister." It's important not to deny what the child is feeling toward her or his sibling. You might say, "It sure sounds like you're upset with Susan." **Young people (and adults) need to be able to express their feelings and have them recognized.** Try to listen without feeling you have to take sides.

Encourage positive communication between your children. Have them set aside time for each other just to talk. Spend time talking together as a family—and be sure everyone gets heard. Teach your children a "feelings vocabulary," so they know how to talk about what they feel without making accusations.

FAMILY BOUNDARIES

Sibling rivalry may seem to be unavoidable, but **you can help the situation by setting some ground rules.** Obviously, you don't want to see your children physically harmed. You may want to set house rules about play fighting, wrestling, and tickling that make it clear that those activities occur only if both children consider them fun. But there should also be firm limits about verbal exchanges. For example, you might have a rule that name-calling isn't an acceptable way to express anger.

PEACEFUL CONFLICT RESOLUTION

Even siblings who get along are bound to have conflicts at one time or another. When arguments do occur, **it's important not to take sides in sibling fights.** The more parents stay out of minor fights, the more likely it is that children will learn to settle differences on their own.

In most cases, you can ignore normal bickering. But if the situation gets to the point where someone could be physically or emotionally hurt, or your children's own attempts at problem solving fail, then clearly you need to get involved.

When you have to step in, be calm and direct. Acknowledge their anger and give each child a chance to speak. Listen carefully to what they have to say, then see if you can summarize the problem for them. Ask them how they think the situation should be resolved. If they can't come up with a good solution, give them some time apart to think it over. Then get back together as a family and talk about it again. You may want to suggest that the issue of debate be put on the agenda for your next family meeting. Enough time will have passed to talk in an unheated way, or the issue may simply have gone away.

FAMILY SUPPORT

Sometimes you can unintentionally compare one child to the other. Doing this can lower a child's self-esteem and increase jealousy and envy. It's normal to like or appreciate different characteristics or traits in each child, and to find others irritating because they're either too similar to or different from your own. Whatever the case, it's important to **recognize each child's unique talents and encourage their interests even if they don't match yours.** Attend their games and performances and find ways to let them know what you love and admire about them. If your son is good at playing an instrument, go to his performances and compliment him on his talent. If your daughter is good at soccer, go to her games and congratulate her on how skilled she is. Help each child discover and nurture her or his own talents and affirm them in the family. Also, try to put aside time every day to be alone with each child. This helps them to know that they are important as individuals.

INTERPERSONAL COMPETENCE

Knowing how to get along with others is key to helping brothers and sisters live in harmony. **Model good relationships with your siblings.** Have family discussions about relationships; you can talk about the major impact siblings have on each other's self-esteem. If young people know this information, they may be inclined to be more careful about what they say and do. When your children do things that hurt one another's feelings, talk with them about how their behavior affects others.

THE ESSENTIAL TOOLS

The fights happen for a variety of reasons—attention-seeking, jealousy, competition, teasing—and trying to keep the peace in a family can be a challenge. But if we show our children that we love them for who they are and help them learn how to communicate well and resolve conflict, we will give them the essential tools to handle other important relationships in their future.

TV

Your Dilemma:

**"Jamie just sits in front of the TV when he gets home from school.
He barely even says hello. He just goes for that remote."**

or

**"That show Erin watches is all about sex. Sure, the characters are teenagers.
But they're all teenagers having sex!"**

ACTION TIPS

◆ Set clear boundaries on the amount and type of television your children watch.

◆ Consider moving the TV to a less central location in your home.

◆ As a family, talk about the TV shows you watch. Discuss the effects of TV on what you buy, how you talk, and what you think.

◆ Model "responsible viewing" by limiting your own TV time.

◆ Encourage your children to read for pleasure, take part in physical and creative activities, and participate in youth programs that foster positive, real interaction with other young people.

◆ Turn off the TV at least one night a week and bring out some board games to play as a family.

WHAT YOUNG PEOPLE SAY:
"If children are raised well and healthy, they should be free to do anything with their time; they WILL make constructive decisions based upon their personal situations."

Sometimes it seems as though TV is an alien life form that has taken over our homes. For the most part, televisions seem harmless creatures; in fact, they can be perfectly charming. They're chatty little things, spinning out endless stories from morning till night. In the United States, they're even a cultural connection to the outside world for some families who do not speak much English. But TV programming can also be violent, inane, or just plain loud. The most disturbing aspect, though, is the way these machines command the family's attention, sometimes even seeming to rob people of the power of speech. Young people seem especially susceptible to their influence, often sitting in front of the TV for hours on end, transfixed.

As an occasional form of entertainment, TV can be fun and relaxing. But as a way of life, zoning out in front of the tube is nothing short of mind-numbing. Unfortunately, the television has become the center of many homes, and its incessant drone fills up the space between family members, creating distance where there used to be connection. When TV assumes too great a role in young people's lives (or in your life), a sense of alienation from other people is almost inevitable, and the hypnotic effects of TV can drain their (or your) time and energy for other activities.

Fortunately, television is relatively easy to put in its place. The developmental assets are positive qualities, experiences, and skills that children need to grow up healthy and responsible. Parents, grandparents, stepparents, or any other guardian of a child can use these assets as a framework to help them think through the new experiences they're encountering with their children. When dealing with TV issues, the assets you may want to consider looking at for guidance are Family Boundaries, Adult Role Models, Positive Family Communication, Reading for Pleasure, Creative Activities, and Youth Programs.

ASSET TYPE	ASSET NAME	ASSET DESCRIPTION
Support	Family Boundaries	Parents set clear rules and consequences for their children's behavior. They monitor their children's whereabouts.
Boundaries and Expectations	Adult Role Models	Parents and other adults model positive, responsible behavior.
Support	Positive Family Communication	Young people turn to their parents for advice and support. They have frequent, in-depth conversations with each other on a variety of topics. Parents are approachable and available when their children want to talk.
Commitment to Learning	Reading for Pleasure	Young people read for pleasure three or more hours per week.
Constructive Use of Time	Creative Activities	Young people spend three or more hours each week in lessons or practice in music, theater, or other arts.
Constructive Use of Time	Youth Programs	Young people spend three or more hours per week in sports, clubs, or organizations at school and/or in the community.

FAMILY BOUNDARIES

Set clear boundaries on the amount and type of television your children watch. Explain why these boundaries are important. For example, if you are limiting their viewing of shows that are violent or that trade on themes of sexual exploitation, explain why you consider these inappropriate.

If the television is displayed prominently in your home—in the living room, for example—consider moving it to a more remote part of the house if possible. **Putting the TV in a less central location sends an important message that it isn't going to be the focal point of your home life.** If it's in your budget, you might even think about getting a smaller set that can be stored in a closet when not in use. Certainly, resist buying a TV for every bedroom.

ADULT ROLE MODELS

What TV signals are your adolescents getting from you? Many families have the television on almost all the time. It plays in the background during family meals. It continues on while people talk on the phone or even together in the living room. Think about your own TV use and any changes you may want to make that will make a difference in the effect TV has on how *you* live.

POSITIVE FAMILY COMMUNICATION

Talking about TV and its impact on our lives can actually be a lot more interesting than watching it. There's no denying the effect TV has on our view of the world, the way we talk and dress, and the objects we want to buy. Learning to pay attention to how television "programs" our thinking can be an interesting way to develop critical thinking skills.

Talk about the programs your family does watch, and start to notice the messages they send. Pay attention to commercials, too. Make a game of it. Identify where certain phrases or expressions come from, which show introduced a certain hairstyle, who the real audience for products are, and what products you or your children urgently want to buy because of a slick commercial. If a certain show or ad strikes you as particularly offensive, talk about it together and write a letter to the network or the company that produced it.

READING FOR PLEASURE

Let reading assume a more prominent role in your family's life. Keep interesting books and magazines around the house, and talk about what each of you is currently reading. **Encourage your children to read almost anything, even comic books and cartoons.** Read books, magazines, or newspaper articles aloud to each other. Try to find books that are tied to movies or television shows and read them as a family, then discuss them together. (For example, you might watch the movie *Clueless* together, and then read *Emma*, the Jane Austen novel on which it was based.)

Go to the library together, and encourage your older children to volunteer there, reading to younger children. If possible, put bookcases in your children's rooms, so they can fill them with their favorite books. Give your children inscribed copies of books you loved when you were their age. When it's time for your children to receive gifts, ask others to give them books as presents.

CREATIVE ACTIVITIES

Open up the world of the imagination for your children. **Encourage them in artistic pursuits,** such as taking music lessons, drawing, painting, acting, and writing. Share your excitement about a particular artist or work of art. Spend time as a family

- listening to music (share your favorite CDs or cassettes);

- going to art museums (most museums have a free day);

- working on art projects (for example, create a family scrapbook with a section about each person's interests, friends, story of how their name was chosen, and life story);

- attending concerts, plays, movies, and cultural events (high school events are free or inexpensive).

- renting movies or TV shows about artists and musicians, or watching televised performances and concerts.

YOUTH PROGRAMS

Involvement in youth programs provides a sense of belonging to a group and also helps young people reduce their reliance on television for entertainment. The more "plugged in" they are in a positive way with other people their age, the less likely they are to want to sit around watching TV. **The after-school hours are prime TV time for many youth—especially if they're home alone—so this is an important time for structured activities.**

Encourage your children to get involved in youth programs sponsored by the school, community, or your place of worship. These might include clubs (such as chess, photography, or book clubs), athletic teams, culturally specific youth groups, and organizations such as 4H, Scouts, or Camp Fire USA.

Emphasize the importance of regular physical activity.
Take family bike rides, shoot some hoops, or just go for a walk together. Find out what kind of organized sports are available in your area that your child might be interested in. If your child isn't interested in athletics, look into dance, karate, or yoga classes, or check out the other programs available for adolescents at your local YWCA or YMCA, Boys and Girls Club, Camp Fire USA, recreation center, etc.

LOSING THE REMOTE

Young people need to be out living life, not sitting in a dark room watching TV. (So do the rest of us.) The more we can help them find meaningful connections in their daily lives—with other people, with nature, with books and music and art—the less likely they are to look to their favorite alien for solace and entertainment. By turning off the TV, we're giving our young people the quiet they need to hear life calling.

Reasons to Get Off the Couch

Getting away from the TV can be a good thing. Asset #17, Creative Activities, encourages adolescents to spend three or more hours per week involved in music, theatre, or other arts. Here are 15 reasons you can give your children for moving off the couch and moving into the arts.

When you're involved in the arts, you:

1. Build skills in creative, complex, and critical thinking; problem solving; risk taking; decision making; flexibility; team work; analysis; explanation; judgment; and communication.

2. Become more creative, insightful, resilient, inventive, original, sensitive, and imaginative.

3. Build self-discipline and self-esteem.

4. Use all of your different kinds of intelligence and preferred learning styles. (If language and logic-mathematic intelligences—the ones on which schools focus most—aren't your strengths, the arts give you other ways to succeed and achieve.)

5. Learn to find structure and meaning where none seem to exist (e.g., when you make sense out of seemingly random movements in a dance, or shapes in a painting, or notes in a piece of music).

6. Learn to cope with uncertainty (e.g., how will this color look? how will that note sound? what if I read the lines in a play this way instead of that way?).

7. Learn to deal with ambiguity. (Arithmetic, spelling, reading, and punctuation all depend on specific rules to obtain the right answers, but there are no right answers in creating or interpreting art.)

8. Discover, appreciate, and understand different cultures and cultural values, and feel more connected to your own culture.

9. Acquire knowledge and meaning you don't get from other subjects (e.g., an artist's interpretation of love, birth,   death, or conflict).

10. Enhance your performance in other subjects. (Drawing helps writing; songs and poems make facts memo rable;   drama makes history vivid and real; creative movement makes processes understandable; sound, movement, space, line, shape, and color are all related to math and science.)

11. Gain insight into people, ideas, events, and experiences that aren't part of your normal life.

12. Get more involved in learning because art makes learning more fun. (The arts = *doing*, not just passively taking in information.)

13. Learn ways to cope with the ups and downs of adolescence. (The arts give you positive, healthy ways to express conflicting emotions and get a handle on them.)

14. Gain a different perspective on your life—a chance to imagine a different outcome and develop a critical distance from everyday life. (If your life isn't the greatest, the arts are a way to cope.)

15. Improve your ability to think and create. These are talents many businesses look for in a person. Many prominent business leaders have argued that economic success depends on the competencies provided by a solid education in the arts.

The Internet

Your Dilemma:

**"It seems like Sydney's on the computer 24/7.
She never gets outside or reads a book anymore."**
or
**"I'm worried about Julio.
I think he may have 'met' someone older online."**

ACTION TIPS

◆ Set positive boundaries regarding use of the Internet. Emphasize what you hope your children will get out of their surfing.

◆ Use the Internet as a way for your children to meet young people from other countries. This can be a positive learning experience.

◆ Keep the computer in an area of the house where the family gathers regularly. Use the Internet as a tool for gathering information and facilitating discussion. Ask your kids which sites catch their eye and why.

◆ Provide your children with guidance about Internet safety, especially in chat rooms.

◆ Have a talk together about honesty on the Internet and the temptation to misrepresent oneself.

◆ Encourage your children to participate in art programs, sports, or youth organizations. Join some clubs yourself to set a good example.

◆ Find out what the Internet policies are at your local library and at your children's school.

WHAT YOUNG PEOPLE SAY: "Parents inquire and restrict because they care, but parents who care also allow for personal growth, learning, and fun, too."

We live in an electronic age. TVs, radios, video games, and computers all vie for our young people's time. There's no doubt that the Internet is an amazing portal to learning and exploring opportunities. But the Web also has a darker side—e.g., the array of pornography readily available, the stories of pedophiles preying on children in chat rooms. Not to mention the Internet's "gray" side; at times, it seems no better than TV, simply sucking away time in sedentary activity.

How do we monitor our children's time on the Internet without making them feel we're interfering? Sure, Web filters and online services are one way to help protect our children from the Internet's negative influences. But they're certainly no cure-all, and sometimes they actually block young people from good content designed especially for them.

The developmental assets are positive qualities, experiences, and skills that children need to grow up healthy and responsible. Parents, grandparents, stepparents, or any other guardian of a child can use these assets as a framework to help them think through the new experiences they're encountering with their children. When dealing with Internet issues, the assets and larger asset categories you may want to consider looking at for guidance are Family Boundaries, Cultural Competence, Positive Family Communication, Safety, Honesty, Constructive Use of Time, and Support.

ASSET TYPE	ASSET NAME	ASSET DESCRIPTION
Boundaries and Expectations	Family Boundaries	Parents set clear rules and consequences for their children's behavior. They monitor their children's whereabouts.
Social Competencies	Cultural Competence	Young people know and are comfortable with people of different cultural, racial, and/or ethnic backgrounds.
Support	Positive Family Communication	Young people turn to their parents for advice and support. They have frequent, in-depth conversations with each other on a variety of topics. Parents are approachable and available when their children want to talk.
Empowerment	Safety	Young people feel safe at home, at school, and in their neighborhood.
Positive Values	Honesty	Young people tell the truth even when it's not easy.
Constructive Use of Time	Asset #17 Creative Activities Asset #18 Youth Programs Asset #19 Religious Community Asset #20 Time at Home	Young people need constructive, enriching opportunities for growth through creative activities, youth programs, congregational involvement, and quality time at home.
Support	Asset #1 Family Support Asset #2 Positive Family Communication Asset #3 Other Adult Relationships Asset #4 Caring Neighborhood Asset #5 Caring School Climate Asset #6 Parent Involvement in Schooling	Young people need to experience support, care, and love from their families and many others. They need organizations and institutions that provide positive, supportive environments.

FAMILY BOUNDARIES

It's important to set specific boundaries regarding Internet use. Make sure you and any other involved adult guardian agree on what is appropriate for your children. Boundaries work when adults stand together. **When you set boundaries, put a positive spin on them and tell your children not only what you don't want them to do but also what you want them to do and why.** For example, encourage them to use the Internet to check out stuff on their favorite bands and to chat with friends using instant messaging.

Check in monthly to discuss the boundaries you've set. Do they seem fair and appropriate to both you and your children? Be prepared to make adjustments. Perhaps you've agreed to set an alarm clock so your children don't lose track of time; maybe you'll allow an extra 10 minutes a few days a week if they finish all their homework.

Consider not having a computer with Internet access in your adolescent's room. Having the computer more centrally located makes it easier to monitor your child's use and reduces time spent on the computer, as well as the resulting isolation.

CULTURAL COMPETENCE

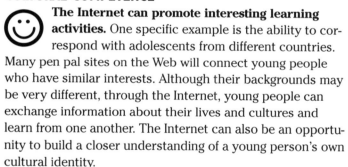

The Internet can promote interesting learning activities. One specific example is the ability to correspond with adolescents from different countries. Many pen pal sites on the Web will connect young people who have similar interests. Although their backgrounds may be very different, through the Internet, young people can exchange information about their lives and cultures and learn from one another. The Internet can also be an opportunity to build a closer understanding of a young person's own cultural identity.

POSITIVE FAMILY COMMUNICATION

There are many ways **you can make the Internet a positive, family-oriented activity.** For example, keep the computer in the kitchen, living room, or another busy area of the house. If your children know more about computers than you do (which may very well be true), sit down together and let them teach you some of what they know. Ask them to teach you search skills or to help you with a project. Maybe they could find parks, museums, or other interesting free places for your family to visit.

Stay in touch with what your children are doing online. Ask them about their favorite Web sites. Use the Internet as a way to discuss important issues with your children. Spend some time surfing the net together.

If your children report that they find something disturbing on the Internet, don't blame them. Be supportive and, instead, give them guidance and help them to avoid future problems. **Talking with young people about safety on the Internet is extremely important.**

SAFETY

Most of the time the Internet is a place for learning, education, and fun. But sometimes it can be a dangerous place. Shy adolescents may like the Internet because they find it easier to talk to people online than in person. But chat rooms, if not monitored, can lead to trouble. **Adolescents should be instructed and reminded never to give out personal information anywhere on the Internet.** They shouldn't tell chat room visitors anything about their families or where they live. Most often this information is used for advertising purposes, but from time to time it's used to start harmful relationships. Also, tell your children not to set up meetings with people they encounter on the Internet.

HONESTY

Misrepresentations are abundant on the Internet, both of information and identity. Have a family discussion about why people claim to be someone they're not on the Internet. This may lead to a good talk about self-esteem. **Teach them not to believe without question everything they see online,** and discuss situations in which adolescents suspect people or Web sites may have been dishonest. Encourage your children to be honest about themselves but self-protective, too.

CONSTRUCTIVE USE OF TIME

If you feel your children are spending too much time on the Internet, help **get them involved in creative activities and youth programs.** For example, let them choose a creative activity to get involved in— maybe playing the drums, acting, or drawing. Talk with your children about their interests. Then help them locate teams, classes, clubs, or organizations that fit those interests. You can even set a good example by getting involved with a team, club, or organization that interests you.

When your children are on the Internet, **encourage them to seek out sites that relate to their own hobbies and interests.** They might look for sites that feature their favorite musicians, writers, or other celebrities. If neither you nor your children know much about the Internet, take a class and learn about it together.

SUPPORT

Other people around you may be able to help give you guidance regarding the Internet. Ask teachers, librarians, and other Internet users in your neighborhood if you're concerned about your children's Internet use. Also, find out what the Internet policy is at your local library and at your children's school.

A USEFUL TOOL

Although the Internet contains its share of pitfalls, it's too useful to be ignored. Hundreds of new Web sites are added to the Internet every day—some of them good, some of them bad. And even good ones can go bad, when owners of domain names change. But among the good are sources of reference information and means of communication. You and your children can find news, weather, movie reviews, encyclopedias, as well as school and health information online. When used with care, the Internet can be fun, safe, and educational.

An Internet Safety Checklist

You might want to begin a conversation about Internet safety by telling your children that their safety is important to you. And to keep them safe, they should follow these boundaries. You can even clip these tips and post them by your family's computer.

Remember . . .

- to keep personal information private. This means not giving out my address, phone number, and the name and location of my school.

- to keep my passwords secret, even from friends.

- to use a nickname in chat rooms, that way I can exit if someone makes me uncomfortable and my screen name won't make me easy to trace.

- to never send anyone my photo without checking with mom or dad first.

- to let my parents know right away if I come across any information that makes me uncomfortable.

- to never agree to get together in person with anyone I "meet" online without making sure it's okay with my parents. If they say it's okay, only meet in a public place and bring mom or dad along.

- to never respond to any mean or hurtful messages and to never write any threats, which is breaking the law.

• Internet Safety Checklist adapted from National Center for Missing and Exploited Children.
• This handout is intended to provide parents with a positive approach to common parenting concerns. It is not intended to take the place of appropriate counseling or other professional help in serious situations.
• **Developmental assets help youth and their parents thrive.** To learn more about what assets can do for your family, visit www.search-institute.org or ask a parent educator in your community. •
• From *When Parents Ask for Help: Everyday Issues through an Asset-Building Lens,* copyright © 2003 by Search Institute, 800-888-7828. This handout may be reproduced for educational, noncommercial uses only (with this copyright line). All rights reserved.

Chores

Your Dilemma:

"His room is a disaster. All I ask is to see the carpet again."
or
"Sheila's got homework *and* softball practice keeping her busy during the week. Is it too much to ask for help with dinner on Sunday night?"

ACTION TIPS

◆ Have a family discussion about chores to decide who will do what and when.

◆ Evenly distribute tasks that are sometimes stereotyped by gender.

◆ Set standards for each chore. By doing a job together with your children the first few times, you can show them how you would like it done.

◆ Create a checklist or chart to keep track of everyone's chores.

◆ Show your children a good example by modeling responsibility and following through on your own chores.

◆ Do big chores together as a family and make them a fun event by doing them to every one's favorite music or by ordering pizza or watching a movie together afterward.

◆ Always compliment your children for being helpful and for doing good work. Positive feedback is always encouraging.

◆ Help your children get started with a job if it's a new one.

◆ Set time limits so no one works too long.

FACT: In 1976, 41 percent of 12th-grade students performed daily household chores; in 1999, only 24 percent reported doing daily household chores.

From: DoleSalads.com

Chores. It's an ugly word in most every household. Hardly anyone likes to do them, but they have to get done. Otherwise, there may not be clean clothes to wear to school or work. The last sheet of toilet paper may dangle from the roll, and there may be more food under the couch cushions than inside the refrigerator.

Chores teach adolescents a variety of life lessons. They learn the importance of cooperation and self-reliance. They also gain the confidence they need to live an independent life. And handling chores among their other responsibilities teaches them valuable planning and scheduling skills.

So how do we help our children learn to embrace this less-than-thrilling aspect of daily life?

The developmental assets are positive qualities, experiences, and skills that children need to grow up healthy and responsible. Parents, grandparents, stepparents, or any other guardian of a child can use these assets as a framework to help them think through the new experiences they're encountering with their children. When dealing with the issue of chores in your family, the assets and larger asset categories you may want to consider looking at for guidance are Positive Family Communication, Family Boundaries, Responsibility, Family Support, and Empowerment.

ASSET TYPE	ASSET NAME	ASSET DESCRIPTION
Support	Positive Family Communication	Young people turn to their parents for advice and support. They have frequent, in-depth conversations with each other on a variety of topics. Parents are approachable and available when their children want to talk.
Boundaries and Expectations	Family Boundaries	Parents set clear rules and consequences for their children's behavior. They monitor their children's whereabouts.
Positive Values	Responsibility	Young people accept and take personal responsibility for their actions and decisions.
Support	Family Support	Young people feel loved and supported in their family.
Empowerment	Asset #7 Community Values Youth Asset #8 Youth as Resources Asset #9 Service to Others Asset #10 Safety	Young people need to be valued by their community and have opportunities to contribute to others. For this to occur, they must be safe and feel secure.

POSITIVE FAMILY COMMUNICATION

The first step in dealing with chores is discussing them. You can create a climate in which chores are expected, a part of family life. You may want to ask that people pick two different chores to do each week. That way, your children learn many life skills but still feel included in the decision making. When discussing how chores will be done, acknowledge everyone's busy schedules and say how much you appreciate and value the help in keeping the household running smoothly.

Assigning chores can be a good time to talk about gender roles. **Girls and boys should share the same tasks and not be given certain duties because of their gender.** Girls can do basic repairs and yard work, and boys can do cooking and laundry. Both girls and boys need to know how to do each of these jobs.

FAMILY BOUNDARIES

For each chore, set standards, but explain each job as well. **The first couple of times your child does a task, do it together.** That way, you can show how to do it—don't assume your adolescent will know. Demonstrating how to do a chore will also give you the opportunity to show the quality of work you expect to see when finished. You may want to make up a checklist for each chore so that your child knows exactly what needs to be accomplished each time he or she does the job.

A young person's mind is rarely on doing chores. You can try several different techniques as gentle reminders. **Create a reminder sheet of chores for everyone in the home to do,** including you. Another option is to ask your child to keep track of each family member's success with chores.

RESPONSIBILITY

Chores are an excellent way to teach young people responsibility. They learn to become an integral part of a smooth-running household. This will be invaluable when they move out and live with other roommates or on their own. Model responsibility in your daily life. **Make an effort to get your own chores done.**

Adolescents are at an age when they can be helpful in many areas. Here are just some of the chores that are appropriate for this age-group:

- Meal preparation: budgeting and shopping for meals; cooking; setting and clearing the table; serving; cleaning up.

- Cleaning: of their own room; of family areas, including bathroom and kitchen; straightening up, dusting, vacuuming.

- Laundry: sorting by color; washing and drying; folding; putting away.

- Maintenance: yard work; painting; simple repairs; car maintenance.

- Child care: help with younger brothers and sisters.

- Pet care.

- Car washing.

- Recycling.

FAMILY SUPPORT

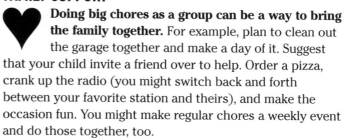

Doing big chores as a group can be a way to bring the family together. For example, plan to clean out the garage together and make a day of it. Suggest that your child invite a friend over to help. Order a pizza, crank up the radio (you might switch back and forth between your favorite station and theirs), and make the occasion fun. You might make regular chores a weekly event and do those together, too.

Encourage your children and everyone in the family to do little things daily. This teaches basic thoughtfulness. If the trashcan is full, empty it. If you use the last of the toilet paper, get out a fresh roll.

And remember to **praise your adolescent for doing a good job** or to point out when he or she is being helpful. It's always nice to feel appreciated.

EMPOWERMENT

Doing chores emphasizes that young people have useful roles within the family. They help make the family work. Talk with your children about how their contributions help the family, and thank them for their support.

A JOB WELL DONE

From time to time, chores might still be met with reluctance. After all, nobody's perfect. But overall, successful accomplishment of chores helps adolescents learn to be functioning members of a household. They learn responsibility, cooperation, and self-reliance. Once they move on to life after high school, they'll be grateful for the basic living skills you've taught them. Because once they're on their own, they'll learn chores are just part of the deal.

Curfew

Your Dilemma:

**"Mom, I'm going out with Darnel and the guys. I'll be home later.
Maybe around midnight, I'm not sure. See you, bye."**

or

**"Tanya just turned 15. She wants to start staying out until midnight
on Saturdays. I don't know what to do."**

ACTION TIPS

◆ Talk together with your children when deciding on routine curfews. Try to come to a reasonable compromise.

◆ Set and enforce consequences for breaking curfew. For example, if a young person comes home 30 minutes late, the next time he or she goes out, that child will have to come home an hour early.

◆ Be sure your children know ahead of time what the consequences of breaking curfew are.

◆ For safety reasons, ask children where they plan on being. Have them call home if they change locations.

◆ Compliment your children when they make curfew and when they keep you informed of where they're going to be.

◆ Model being considerate. When you go out, let your children know where you're going and when you hope to be home.

WHAT YOUNG PEOPLE SAY: "I'd be happy to let my mom know where I am if she'd just let me go places and be willing to negotiate new rules with me."

Adolescence is a time when children want to assert their independence. And what better way than staying out late, hanging out with friends away from home? But at the same time, our children are not yet adults and still need our protection and guidance. For these reasons, curfew can become a hot-button topic in many families.

The developmental assets are positive qualities, experiences, and skills that children need to grow up healthy and responsible. Parents, grand-parents, stepparents, or any other guardian of a child can use these assets as a framework to help them think through the new experiences they're encountering with their children. When dealing with the issue of curfew in your family, the assets you may want to consider looking at for guidance are Positive Family Communication, Family Boundaries, Safety, Responsibility, and Adult Role Models.

ASSET TYPE	ASSET NAME	ASSET DESCRIPTION
Support	Positive Family Communication	Young people turn to their parents for advice and support. They have frequent, in-depth conversations with each other on a variety of topics. Parents are approachable and available when their children want to talk.
Boundaries and Expectations	Family Boundaries	Parents set clear rules and consequences for their children's behavior. They monitor their children's whereabouts.
Empowerment	Safety	Young people feel safe at home, at school, and in their neighborhood.
Positive Values	Responsibility	Young people accept and take personal responsibility for their actions and decisions.
Boundaries and Expectations	Adult Role Models	Parents and other adults model positive, responsible behavior.

POSITIVE FAMILY COMMUNICATION

Ask for your children's input when deciding on curfews. **See what they think is fair and talk about the issue together.** Come to a compromise if possible. Your children may want midnight, while 10 P.M. may seem much more suitable to you. Perhaps in this case 11 P.M. would be reasonable.

Some curfew decisions are simplified by factors such as time of the local community curfew, time of available public transportation, or your willingness to pick up your children. Routine curfews can be set for weekdays and weekends, but these can be changed for special occasions, such as a big dance. You may also consider changing a curfew time if there will be adult supervision or if your children have done extra chores to earn extra time. As a family, review set curfew times regularly to make sure they are working and acceptable. Adjust curfews together based on your child's age, maturity, and evidence of responsible behavior.

Your child may question why some of his or her friends get to stay out later than he or she does. It's important to have a conversation together not only explaining that your rules may be tighter than those of other families or the community in general but also explaining why you see the need for that difference.

FAMILY BOUNDARIES

It's important for young people to know that there will be consequences for ignoring their curfew. A logical consequence is a more restrictive curfew the next time. You may want to allow a 5- or 10-minute grace period, but after that, they should expect to give up the privilege of staying out late. For example, if they come in at 10:30 instead of 10:00 on Thursday, then on Saturday, they know that they'll have to be in at 10:00 instead of 11:00. Be consistent in enforcing consequences.

Make sure your children are aware of your expectations ahead of time. You may want to review their curfew and the consequences of missing curfew before they go out. You may also want your children to call in if plans change. That way you'll know where they are.

SAFETY

One of the main reasons we set curfews is to keep our young people safe. Get to know your children's friends and their parents. Keep a list of friends' names, their parents' names, addresses, and phone numbers. **Before children go out, find out where they're going to be.** Also ask how they're going to get home and know when they plan to be in. You may suggest that if your children are just going to be walking around with friends that they call in every couple of hours, so you know that they're okay. It might also be a good idea to have them call if they change location. Some young people appreciate having a curfew; it gives them a good excuse for getting out of uncomfortable situations. Check in with your adolescents about keeping themselves safe, and reassure them that if they find themselves in trouble, they can always call you or another adult they trust.

RESPONSIBILITY

Recognize and affirm responsible behavior. **Let your children know that you appreciate when they come home on time and let you know where they are.** If they do come home late occasionally but for good reason, be willing to cut them some slack. As they mature, give adolescents more responsibility. You're preparing them for the discipline of living on their own. You might eventually say, "Try being home by 11, but if you can't make it, please call."

ADULT ROLE MODELS

Keep them informed of your whereabouts when you go out, too. How you role model responsibility is important for setting a standard and showing that thoughtfulness works both ways.

TIME IS ON YOUR SIDE

We set curfews to guide and protect adolescent children. Without it, they would probably stay up all night and sleep all day, missing out on school, sunshine, and daily life. By making young people part of the curfew discussion and establishing clear expectations and consequences, we can give them some of the independence they are looking for at this time in their lives while still maintaining the boundaries they need to thrive.

Family Whereabouts Contract

We, the members of the _____ family, promise to keep each other informed of our whereabouts at all times. This means telling someone in the family:

1. where we'll be,

2. the name(s) of the person(s) we'll be with,

3. a number where we can be reached, and

4. when we'll be back.

Signed on this date _____

By   _____   _____

      _____   _____

      _____   _____

Food

Your Dilemma:

"As soon as he gets home from school, Jesse goes right for the chips and cookies. I think he's allergic to healthy food."

ACTION TIPS

◆ Try to have at least one meal together as a family every day. If that's not possible, aim for at least a few times each week.

◆ Keep the kitchen stocked with healthy snacks.

◆ Make cooking a family event—and a learning opportunity. Explore new kinds of food together; visit a farmers' market or ethnic grocery store.

◆ Share responsibility for shopping and cooking among all members of the household.

◆ Plant a garden together. Increase everyone's appreciation of the food they eat.

◆ Volunteer as a family for a hunger-relief organization.

As anyone who has ever tried to spoon-feed mashed yams into an unhappy toddler can attest, food can become a surprisingly emotional issue between parents and children. And for the parents of adolescents, food can take on a great deal of symbolic weight.

For one thing, it's a pretty safe way for young people to assert their independence. If the family eats meat, they may become vegetarian. Or if the family is vegetarian, they may start eating meat. Adolescents have more authority over their food choices than they did when they were younger, and they're interested in exercising that power.

Something about adolescence also seems to trigger a craving for junk food. Chips, pizza, sweets, and fast food tend to become the major food groups. So getting a decent meal into a young person can be a challenge. Add on the busy schedules of most families, and you've got a recipe for nutritional breakdown.

The developmental assets are positive qualities, experiences, and skills that children need to grow up healthy and responsible. Parents, grandparents, stepparents, or any other guardian of a child can use these assets as a framework to help them think through the new experiences they're encountering with their children. When dealing with food issues, the assets and larger asset categories you may want to consider looking at for guidance are Positive Family Communication, Family Support, and Commitment to Learning.

ASSET TYPE	ASSET NAME	ASSET DESCRIPTION
Support	Positive Family Communication	Young people turn to their parents for advice and support. They have frequent, in-depth conversations with each other on a variety of topics. Parents are approachable when their children want to talk.
Support	Family Support	Young people feel loved and supported in their family.
Commitment to Learning	Asset #21 Achievement Motivation Asset #22 School Engagement Asset #23 Homework Asset #24 Bonding to School Asset #25 Reading for Pleasure	Young people need to develop a lifelong commitment to education and learning.

VE FAMILY COMMUNICATION

Communication is a key ingredient in creating a healthier diet for your family. **Have family discussions about food.** Talk about your likes and dislikes. Ask everyone to make a list of the foods they simply refuse to eat (with a limit of five or so) and a list of their favorite foods. Make some agreements about which foods will not appear on the menu. In our family, this is the No-Brussels Sprouts Clause. In your family, it may be the No-Canned-Peaches Clause. When young people have one of these special food clauses in their contract, be sure to honor it. (No one should be forced to eat food he or she feels is yucky!)

Talk about the importance of sharing meals as a family. **Try to have at least one complete meal together every day.** If this simply isn't possible, work together on arranging your schedules so you can do it several times a week at least. It's worth juggling and rearranging activities to make room for this time together. Family meals give everyone a chance to slow down, share a nutritious meal, and get caught up with each other's lives.

FAMILY SUPPORT

A healthy diet has benefits for the entire family, and it's a lot easier if everyone is in on the plan. Make a commitment together to eating well. Here are some ideas for changing the family's approach to food.

Keep the kitchen stocked with healthy snacks. A big bowl of fresh fruit on the counter and vegetables and dip in the fridge can entice even a confirmed junk-food fiend, especially if other snacks aren't available. Try to limit the purchase of sweets and high-fat, high-sodium foods, such as cookies and chips.

Make cooking a family event. Food preparation doesn't have to be the sole responsibility of one parent. Teaching young people how to cook can be a lot of fun and can be a great opportunity to help them learn to appreciate good nutrition. Some excellent cookbooks specifically designed for young people are available. *Kids Cooking* (Jean Paré, Company's Coming Publishing Ltd., 1995) and *The Quick and Healthy Cookbook* (Brenda J. Ponichtera, Scaledown Publishing, 1994), which has simple recipes for healthy meals, are nice starting points for adolescents. Knowing what goes into a meal makes young people more likely to appreciate meals that other people prepare for them. It also gives them a practical skill that will serve them well when they're out on their own.

Let your children do the cooking one week a month. Give them a reasonable budget to work within, have them plan the dinner menus for the week, do the shopping, and prepare the meals. (You'll probably want to establish some ground rules about buying junk food and about what constitutes a meal. For example, maybe they can make pizza *one* night, but not three.) Suggest they invite a friend over to help them cook or to do the shopping. They may grumble about it at first, but they'll probably end up enjoying it. And they'll learn a lot about what goes into feeding a family. As a variation, have them plan and cook a meal one night per week. To make things interesting, try ethnic themes from time to time.

Plant a garden together. Planting and tending a vegetable garden is a fun and relaxing family activity, and it's a great way to foster a healthy relationship with food. Or, try a spice garden with spices from your family culture. To help adolescents find this activity more appealing, let them have a portion of the garden to plant as they please. See if any of your neighbors are interested in planning a community garden, and create a special part of it just for young people. Encourage older children to help the little ones with planting and weeding.

Consider your own cultural background. Use time around the table and culturally related food to tell stories about your family. Help your children understand food's important connection to your culture.

COMMITMENT TO LEARNING

Food can become a great teaching tool. Learning about food can be a starting point for education about politics, science, anthropology, and economics, just to name a few possibilities. **Help young people see the connections between what they eat and how they feel and perform.** For example, explain how other cultures' low-fat diets mean that their populations have a much lower risk of heart attack than Americans. You can also find ways to explore learning connections in your community.

Visit your local farmers' market. Introduce your children to the farmers. Make it a family project to find out as much as you can about where your food comes from. Invite one of the farmers to come and talk at your children's school.

Plan a neighborhood food fair. Ask each family to prepare a large quantity of a favorite dish to share, maybe something that is traditional in their family. Share recipes, talk about food traditions and nutrition, and enjoy a great potluck meal together.

Check out an ethnic grocery store. Make a family shopping trip to a store that caters to a particular ethnic group that's different from yours. Buy some unfamiliar foods and try them out. You might want to find a recipe ahead of time and get the ingredients while you're there. This is a great way to learn about a culture.

Start a teens' cooking group. If your congregation has a youth group, suggest that they plan some activities that involve learning to prepare nutritious food. Pizza parties are great once in awhile, but they needn't be the staple of every youth program. Young people can have a great time learning to cook together. Or, start a kids-who-cook tradition in your neighborhood, and ask the young people if they would like to prepare a meal for the adults once a month.

Volunteer as a family for a hunger-relief organization. Serving meals to homeless families or raising money to end hunger gives young people a chance to contribute meaningfully to the community. It can also help them appreciate the food they have.

HOME COOKING

One of the primary tasks of parenting is making sure our children are well fed. This can be hard enough when they're 7 and refuse to eat their vegetables. It can be downright exasperating when they're 17 and refuse to eat anything but burgers and fries.

Slowing down young people long enough to get a good meal into them may require a concerted effort. But it's effort well spent. Taking time to sit together and share a meal gives us more than just nutrients. It also gives us a chance to spend time with the people we love, to remember what we appreciate about each other, and to be grateful for all we've been given. Such a break nourishes the family—body and soul.

School and Homework

Your Dilemma:

**"Our daughter, Camryn, seems bored with school.
She doesn't even bring books home to study."**

or

"Pete is overloaded with homework. He can barely keep up."

ACTION TIPS

◆ Be clear about your expectations with regard to school. Expect young people to do their best, but allow them room to make mistakes.

◆ Make lifelong learning part of your family's outlook. Share your enthusiasm for life with your children, and help them discover that learning can be exciting and fun.

◆ Ask open-ended questions about what's happening at school, such as "What challenges you at school?"

◆ Encourage your children to read for the sheer pleasure of it. Keep interesting books and magazines around the house, and visit your local library together. Take turns reading to each other.

◆ Let your children see that their school is important to you, too. Attend school activities and conferences, get involved in the parent organization, help plan a fundraising event. Show interest in what goes on each day at school.

WHAT YOUNG PEOPLE SAY: "I'll know you care about my schoolwork if you come to my teacher conferences (even though I don't really like having those conferences or you being there)."

Education can be seen as a tremendous gift. It's a time in your life that is set aside specifically for learning, when little else is expected of you. Yet, for many young people in this country, school is a chore and a struggle. And in many families, it is a continuous source of conflict.

Education is a complex and contentious issue. People's responses to the educational system are as varied as their backgrounds. Certainly there is much that can be improved upon in our schools. But regardless of our views on education as a whole, the fact remains that school is a central reality of our young people's lives. And as such, we want our young people to get as much out of it as they possibly can.

The developmental assets are positive qualities, experiences, and skills that children need to grow up healthy and responsible. Parents, grandparents, stepparents, or any other guardian of a child can use these assets as a framework to help them think through the new experiences they're encountering with their children. When dealing with the issue of school and homework in your family, the assets and larger asset categories you may want to consider looking at for guidance are High Expectations, Parent Involvement in Schooling, Commitment to Learning, Reading for Pleasure, School Engagement, Homework, Bonding to School, and Sense of Purpose.

ASSET TYPE	ASSET NAME	ASSET DESCRIPTION
Boundaries and Expectations	High Expectations	Parents and teachers encourage young people to do well.
Support	Parent Involvement in Schooling	Parents are actively involved in helping young people succeed in school. They talk with their children about school, sometimes assist with schoolwork, and attend school events.
Commitment to Learning	Asset #21 Achievement Motivation Asset #22 School Engagement Asset #23 Homework Asset #24 Bonding to School Asset #25 Reading for Pleasure	Young people need to develop a lifelong commitment to education and learning.
Commitment to Learning	Reading for Pleasure	Young people read for pleasure three or more hours per week.
Commitment to Learning	School Engagement	Young people are actively engaged in learning.
Commitment to Learning	Homework	Young people do at least one hour of homework every school day.
Commitment to Learning	Bonding to School	Young people care about their school.
Positive Identity	Sense of Purpose	Young people believe that their life has a purpose.

H EXPECTATIONS

Expecting the best from young people is an important way of expressing our belief in them. When we expect our children to do well, they know that we consider them capable. **Be clear and specific about your expectations regarding school.** You might, for example, tell your children that you expect them to complete all of their homework assignments without being reminded, to get to school on time every day, to make positive contributions in their classes and school activities, and to get the best grades they can. Be sure to give recognition for their accomplishments and efforts.

This doesn't mean, however, that there isn't room for making mistakes. When your children don't live up to your expectations, be honest about your disappointment *in their behavior*, and restate your expectations for the future. Avoid making comments that convey a global sense of disappointment in the child, such as "You're so lazy" or "What's the matter with you?" that can hurt a child's self-esteem. If you're particularly upset about the situation, wait to talk to your child until you've had time to calm down.

If your child is struggling in school, try to find out what's at the root of the problem. Ask her or him about what's going on at school, and approach the subject calmly and with compassion. Are the classes too hard? Does your child feel safe at school? Are there social issues that are getting in the way of learning? Is your child depressed? Consider that the root of the problem could also be a learning disability.

Then **find out what additional resources are available to you.** See if your school offers a peer-tutoring or adult-mentoring program, talk to your children's guidance counselor and teachers. Ask about testing for learning disabilities if that seems appropriate. If you think depression may be causing your children's motivation problems, seek the help of a skilled counselor or therapist. Try to keep school from becoming an adversarial issue. Let your children know you want to help make school a positive and exciting part of life.

PARENT INVOLVEMENT IN SCHOOLING

A high predictor of student success is parent involvement in schooling. At least once during the school year, speak with each of your children's teachers. If possible, volunteer time to help out at their school. When you find out about events happening at school, make note of them on the family calendar and attend them.

COMMITMENT TO LEARNING

Even if you aren't comfortable with "book learning," didn't particularly enjoy your school years, or didn't complete your schooling—you have a lot to teach your children. **You can help make learning engaging and stimulating by sharing your own excitement about the world.** Tell them stories about how life was when you were growing up; take them for nature walks; teach them how to do something that you're good at. If English is your second language, teach your children your native tongue. Talk to them about preserving the customs and traditions you grew up with.

Talk to your children about what they're studying in school and try to find ways to support what they're learning. See a local theater production of a play your child is reading in English class. Attend a city council meeting together when your child is studying government. Or, visit an ethnic grocery store that serves an immigrant population your son or daughter is learning about in school. Find ways to approach learning in the spirit of fun and discovery.

Make lifelong learning a high priority in your home. Demonstrate this by exploring new areas of interest, taking a class, and attending lectures and workshops. Have frequent family discussions about ideas and world events. Limit the amount of time you spend watching TV, and look for new and interesting activities to do as a family. Visit an historic site or cultural event in your area, for example, and talk about its significance in local or national history.

READING FOR PLEASURE

For many, the joy of curling up with a good book is one of life's simple pleasures. **Reading is also an important part of a commitment to lifelong learning.** You can encourage your children's appreciation of reading in a number of ways.

- Make regular trips to your local library together. Find out about library-sponsored programs for young people.
- Make books, magazines, and newspapers available in your home. Cut out articles and stories you think might interest your child.
- Choose a book to read together, then discuss it.
- Attend a reading by one of your child's favorite authors.
- Be a role model for reading.
- Start a family book club.

SCHOOL ENGAGEMENT

You can help your children to actively engage in learning in many ways. For example:
- Make sure they eat well and get enough sleep.
- Talk with them every day about what's going on at school.
- Limit the amount of time they spend watching TV.
- Attend school conferences, performances, and other events.

If your adolescent complains about being bored or unhappy at school, take the complaints seriously, and see what can be done to improve the situation. Ask questions: "Do you feel safe at school? Is the work too hard? Too easy? Do you feel that your teachers care about you? Which ones? What about the other students? Do you find it hard to make friends there?" Discuss what you find out with teachers and administrators; work with them and your child to make the school environment more enjoyable and inviting.

HOMEWORK

 Doing at least one hour of homework every school day is one of the assets that helps young people stay on track. Regular study time keeps school high on their list of priorities and makes it less likely that they'll fall behind.

Help your children set up a homework schedule, and plan dinner and other family events around that schedule. A well-lit place for study time is a given, but as far as sound, that's a different story. Some young people work well with a little background noise or soft music. Others may need complete quiet, without the distraction of phone calls or the TV. Provide reference materials for your children to use, such as a dictionary, thesaurus, and desktop encyclopedia. If your children use the Internet for researching a homework assignment, monitor this use occasionally to make sure they are using it for the intended purpose and aren't just "surfing." You might try keeping the computer in the kitchen or another family area. You can also encourage using the library for study or having a study buddy.

If your children are struggling to keep up with homework assignments, or if you're concerned that the assignment load is just too heavy, talk to the teachers right away. Don't wait until your children have fallen so far behind that it's difficult to catch up. Get a written list of missing assignments and anything else your children need to do to get caught up. Then help set up a schedule for completing the missing work while still carrying on with current assignments. (For example, devote one hour a day to "catch-up" work, and a second hour to current work, until the missing assignments are completed.) If your children need additional help, see if peer tutors are available in your school.

If you're concerned that the workload is too heavy, raise this concern with your children's teachers and ask about

eliminating "busy work." Talk to other parents to see whether they're also concerned. Discuss the problem at meetings of the school's parent organization, and talk to the administration to see what can be done.

Offer your support and guidance with homework, and be available to answer questions and review assignments to the best of your ability. If math isn't one of your strengths, maybe there's another caring adult who would be able to help your child. Check in from time to time to see how things are going. Avoid the temptation to get overly involved—i.e., hovering over your children's shoulders or actually doing portions of the work yourself.

BONDING TO SCHOOL

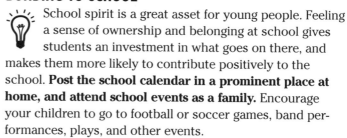 School spirit is a great asset for young people. Feeling a sense of ownership and belonging at school gives students an investment in what goes on there, and makes them more likely to contribute positively to the school. **Post the school calendar in a prominent place at home, and attend school events as a family.** Encourage your children to go to football or soccer games, band performances, plays, and other events.

Contact your children's teachers informally; call them to talk about your children's progress or arrange to visit the school. Make every effort possible to go to conferences. Participate in fundraising events and parent organization activities. Volunteer at the school as a tutor or in some other capacity. Make it clear to your children that their school is important to you, too.

SENSE OF PURPOSE

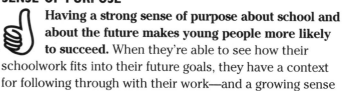 **Having a strong sense of purpose about school and about the future makes young people more likely to succeed.** When they're able to see how their schoolwork fits into their future goals, they have a context for following through with their work—and a growing sense of their ability to accomplish what they set out to do.

THE MEANING OF SCHOOL

School and homework make up a large part of young people's lives. We can support our young people's efforts by showing them that we care as much as they do about what they're getting out of school.

Homework Hints

Here are some tips for you and some ideas to pass along to help your children make the most of their study time.

◆ Provide a place to study that is free of distractions such as television noise and people talking on the phone. (But provide soft music or white noise if it helps your children concentrate.)

◆ Instill a positive attitude. Help your children to think, "I can do this."

◆ Keep all necessary supplies in one place, such as at a desk or computer station. Having pencils, paper, and calculators all in one spot means your children won't have to search for them, which saves time.

◆ Have separate folders for each course to help keep paperwork organized, so it doesn't get lost in the bottom of a backpack.

◆ Establish a regularly scheduled time for doing homework. This time probably should not be immediately after school. Young people need a little time to relax.

◆ Have your children start with the most difficult assignment first.

◆ Let your children take five-minute breaks every so often.

◆ Keep the resources they need available. Start a personal reference library for your children, and keep it current. Begin with the basics: dictionary, thesaurus, almanac, desktop encyclopedia, atlas. Add reference books on specific topics related to your children's classes and interests. If you have a computer, consider buying an encyclopedia on CD-ROM or access online encyclopedias and reference sites.

◆ Encourage your children to study with other students when appropriate.

◆ Remind your children to do as much work as possible during the school day, and if they ride the bus and they feel it's possible, to take advantage of that time to get work done as well.

◆ Recommend that your children keep an assignment notebook so they know what homework must be done each day.

◆ Suggest your children hang on to past quizzes and tests to prepare for future ones.

◆ Encourage your children to make connections between their homework and any cultural or family history.

◆ Praise your children for doing their homework.

◆ Keep in contact with your children's teachers to be aware of the quality and quantity of work being turned in.

Graduation and Beyond

Your Dilemma:

**"It doesn't seem as if Rochelle makes the connection that
what she does today will affect what happens in her future."**
or
**"Wes doesn't seem to have any goals.
And yesterday he said that he doesn't intend to go to college."**

ACTION TIPS

◆ Spend time together as a family. Take the time to enjoy this moment of your lives together, knowing that soon things will change.

◆ Talk about what your child plans to do after graduation. Whether post-secondary education is part of the picture or not, encourage your child to create a plan that suits her or his goals and ambitions.

◆ Gradually increase your child's level of responsibility and freedom. See that he or she has age-appropriate duties around the home.

◆ Help your adolescent learn to manage money. Talk about the importance of creating a budget, setting aside money for fun and for savings, and donating money to worthy causes.

◆ Encourage your child to talk to friends, relatives, and neighbors about the kind of work they do, how they got started in it, and whether they enjoy it. Find out if student internships are available in a field in which your child is interested.

WHAT YOUNG PEOPLE SAY: "Unrealistic dreams and hopes can hurt you sometimes and lead to disappointment; I most appreciate getting help in having a realistic view of the future."

The high school years are a strange borderland between childhood and adulthood. Sometimes our adolescent children can amaze us with their wisdom and maturity; at other times, they can stupefy us with their less-than-mature judgment and defiance. Many young people move out of their parents' home within a couple of years of high school graduation, a move that parents often experience with a mix of joy and sorrow. No matter where they live, they're still our children and take with them all the love and concern that connection brings.

This transition to adulthood is enormous for the entire family. Preparing for it is one of the unifying themes of family life while young people are in high school. In assisting this transition, we often play many roles. We help our children make decisions about work or further education, teach them the skills they need to make it on their own, affirm their sense of connection within the family, and recognize our own need for support.

The developmental assets are positive qualities, experiences, and skills that children need to grow up healthy and responsible. Parents, grandparents, stepparents, or any other guardian of a child can use these assets as a framework to help them think through the new experiences they're encountering with their children. When dealing with the issue of graduation and the future in your family, the assets you may want to consider looking at for guidance are Family Support, Positive Family Communication, Positive View of Personal Future, Responsibility, Planning and Decision Making, Sense of Purpose, Achievement Motivation, High Expectations, and Adult Role Models.

ASSET TYPE	ASSET NAME	ASSET DESCRIPTION
Support	Family Support	Young people feel loved and supported in their family.
Support	Positive Family Communication	Young people turn to their parents for advice and support. They have frequent, in-depth conversations with each other on a variety of topics. Parents are approachable and available when their children want to talk.
Positive Identity	Positive View of Personal Future	Young people are optimistic about their own future.
Positive Values	Responsibility	Young people accept and take personal responsibility for their actions and decisions.
Social Competencies	Planning and Decision Making	Young people know how to plan ahead and make choices.
Positive Identity	Sense of Purpose	Young people believe that their life has a purpose.
Commitment to Learning	Achievement Motivation	Young people are motivated to do well in school.
Boundaries and Expectations	High Expectations	Parents and teachers encourage young people to do well.
Boundaries and Expectations	Adult Role Models	Parents and other adults model positive, responsible behavior.

FAMILY SUPPORT

Helping each other prepare for this next phase of life requires some special attention to your own needs as well as your children's. Strengthening the family's bonds now will help make the transition easier when it comes. Have regular meals together. **Spend time as a family and with your children individually,** and take the time to appreciate these moments in your lives together—because they won't last.

Evaluate your own circumstances to **make sure you have adequate support to carry you through the transition.** Are you satisfied with your job, your friendships, your outside interests? Start thinking about what you can do to make sure you feel happy and excited about your own life as you prepare to send your children off on their next big adventure.

POSITIVE FAMILY COMMUNICATION

Start talking now about what happens after graduation. Share your thoughts and expectations. Ask what ideas and interests your children would like to pursue. Explore various possibilities together. If they are planning to go to college, start thinking about schools. Send for information, check out Web sites together, and talk to people who are familiar with various colleges. If possible, take family trips to visit some of the schools your children are interested in.

If your children don't plan to go to college, find out what they want to do after graduation. Maybe they are interested in a job-training program, internship, or overseas experience. Return to the topic regularly, and encourage your children to keep their options open. **At the same time, emphasize the importance of having a plan.** Young people need to have some sort of vision about their future.

If your children are struggling in school, and you're not sure graduation is even in the picture, try to find out what's at the root of the problem. Ask your children about what's going on at school, and approach the subject calmly and with compassion. Are the classes too hard? Too easy? Do your children feel safe at school? Are there social issues that are getting in the way of learning? Are your children depressed?

Then **find out what additional resources are available to you.** See if your school offers a peer-tutoring or adult-mentoring program, talk to your children's guidance counselor and teachers. Ask about testing for learning disabilities if that seems appropriate. If you think depression may be causing your children's motivation problems, seek the help of a skilled counselor or therapist. Try to keep school from becoming an adversarial issue. Let your children know you want to help make school a positive and exciting part of life.

POSITIVE VIEW OF PERSONAL FUTURE

Foster a sense of optimism about the future in the young people in your life. Look forward to the future with hope and enthusiasm. **Talk about your concerns regarding the future, but frame the discussion positively.** Avoid making negative predictions about what's to come—either in the personal or the global realms.

Affirm your children's dreams (even if they're not your dreams for them), and support their pursuit of them in any way you can. Encourage them to think about their place in the world and how they hope to contribute. Share your own hopes for them in such a way that they feel free to explore their own interests and passions.

RESPONSIBILITY

Gradually increase the number and significance of your child's responsibilities. Post a family-chores chart, and divide up the household tasks according to each person's abilities and schedules. Give children age-appropriate roles in meal preparation, cleanup, laundry, and other daily chores. Make sure each person has a reasonable share of the household duties. Emphasize the importance of working together to keep things running smoothly.

Include conversations about financial responsibility in your family discussions. **Help your adolescents learn about handling money** by teaching them how to balance a checkbook and create a budget. Encourage them to start putting aside money in a savings account and to give some money to causes they care about.

PLANNING AND DECISION MAKING

The high school years are an important time for young people to learn about planning and making careful decisions. **Realize that it may take some time before your child connects what he or she does today with what he or she can or cannot do tomorrow.** Most adolescents eventually make the developmental leap, though some may have narrowed options with poor grades and test scores, and may have to do some catch-up work to pursue their dreams.

Do what you can to help them learn how to plan their homework assignments and work out their schedules so they have time to accomplish what they need to. Developing good time-management skills now will be of great help to them throughout their lives.

Encourage your children to work through the process of making careful decisions. Emphasize the importance of gathering information first. Help them explore potential consequences. Ask them questions that will help them see the issue from various perspectives. Then suggest they weigh the options and make a list of the pros and cons. For example, a decision about buying a car could be broken down into:

- A research phase, in which they investigate cost, safety ratings, and other features of various cars and compare insurance costs.

- A discussion phase, in which they really consider whether they need a car. What might they have to give up in order to make it happen? Do they earn enough at their part-time job?

- An evaluation phase, in which they make lists of pros and cons.

- The final decision, based on what they've learned.

SENSE OF PURPOSE

As a family, **talk about the importance of having a sense of purpose in life.** Share your feelings about what is meaningful in your own life. Ask your children what gives them a sense of purpose and what they hope to accomplish in their lives. Discuss the values you hope they carry with them, such as service to others and concern for social justice. Ask them how these values might be expressed in how they live their lives—the education they seek, the jobs and careers they choose, and the goals they set for themselves. One idea is to have your children write or draw their dreams for the future; then seal these in an envelope. Tell them you'll keep it safe until they finish high school; then, bring it out and remind them to pursue their dreams.

ACHIEVEMENT MOTIVATION

Make it clear to your children that you value learning. Demonstrate this in your own life by learning new things, taking classes, going to museums. Share your excitement about what you learn with your children.

At the same time, **encourage them to follow their own interests.** Avoid imposing your own specific plan on your children. If they have a plan that seems well thought out and reasonable, give them your support, even if the idea differs from the course you had been hoping they might pursue.

HIGH EXPECTATIONS

 You can be open to a variety of possibilities for your children and still have high expectations. Just **let them know you expect them to do their best,** no matter what they decide to do. Believe in their abilities, admire their talents, and encourage them to go for what they want. Give them room to dream big dreams.

ADULT ROLE MODELS

 Encourage your children to connect with people in various fields. They can have simple conversations with friends, neighbors, and relatives for the purpose of learning about different ways of earning a living. Suggest that your children ask these people what's involved in their work, how they got into it, and whether they enjoy what they do. Your children might even be able to arrange to spend some time visiting various workplaces.

If your children have a strong interest in a particular field, see if you can help **arrange an informational interview** for them with someone in that line of work. Or find out if student internships are available in that field. Such positions can help give young people the opportunity to learn firsthand whether they want to pursue a particular course.

PREPARING FOR THE LAUNCH

Our children will still be our children, even when they are out on their own. We will continue to teach, guide, and (probably) annoy them throughout our lives. But the time we have with them while they're still at home is undeniably precious. As we help them prepare for their life journey, we can make sure they carry with them a profound sense of connection with the love and acceptance of home.

Bullying / Being Bullied

Your Dilemma:

**"Mike doesn't want to go to school, and he says he feels ill all the time.
I'm worried that something's going on."**

or

**"I just got a call from an upset parent.
Kendra told some really nasty lies about another girl at school."**

ACTION TIPS

◆ Make sure your child knows that he or she can come to you about anything at anytime.

◆ Report the situation to the school immediately. Afterward, check in with your child to make sure the problem has been solved.

◆ Teach your adolescent resistance skills such as avoiding or ignoring the bully, using humor, walking confidently, and speaking assertively.

◆ If your child is bullying others, seek help from a teacher, principal, or doctor right away.

◆ Promote a policy of telling the truth in your family.

◆ Establish an atmosphere of mutual caring and trust within your home.

◆ Have a young person who has bullied someone take responsibility for her or his actions.

◆ If your child is a bully's target, assure your child that the bullying is not her or his fault, and do other things to boost her or his self-esteem.

◆ Keep the lines of communication open with the staff and faculty of your adolescent's school. Notify them if you have concerns about young people's safety.

◆ Ask your school if they have a bully-prevention policy. If not, help them develop one.

WHAT YOUNG PEOPLE SAY: "Try to be a good role model to kids who are bullies." **AND** "Some people don't like it when other people are unique, but there is no perfect person out there, so everybody should accept how everyone is."

Most people have some unique feature that marks them as "different." For some people, the distinguishing feature might be their super curly hair. For others, it might be those shiny new braces. For some, the factor might not be so visible, such as practicing a different religion than most of the neighbors. Whatever that difference is, it may make them a target for bullies. And whether your child is the bully or the victim, that means trouble.

Bullies and bullying can come in different forms. Some bullies may be loud and outward about their behavior. Other bullies are more subversive and choose to bully through such quiet behavior as spreading lies. A victim may be targeted by a single bully or by an entire group.

Young people who are bullied go through true mental anguish that can disrupt their social and emotional development and affect their school performance. Some find the pain so unbearable, they attempt suicide. What can you do to help your child in this situation? What can you do if your child is on the opposite end and he or she is the one doing the bullying?

The developmental assets are positive qualities, experiences, and skills that children need to grow up healthy and responsible. Parents, grandparents, stepparents, or any other guardian of a child can use these assets as a framework to help them think through the new experiences they're encountering with their children. Whether your family is dealing with the issue of bullying or being bullied, the assets you may want to consider looking at for guidance are Positive Family Communication, Safety, Resistance Skills, Self-Esteem, Caring, Responsibility, Honesty, Family Support, and Caring School Climate.

ASSET TYPE	ASSET NAME	ASSET DESCRIPTION
Support	Positive Family Communication	Young people turn to their parents for advice and support. They have frequent, in-depth conversations with each other on a variety of topics. Parents are approachable and available when their children want to talk.
Empowerment	Safety	Young people feel safe at home, at school, and in their neighborhood.
Social Competencies	Resistance Skills	Young people can resist negative peer pressure and avoid dangerous situations.
Positive Identity	Self-Esteem	Young people feel good about themselves.
Positive Values	Caring	Young people place high value on helping other people.
Positive Values	Responsibility	Young people accept and take personal responsibility for their actions and decisions.
Positive Values	Honesty	Young people tell the truth even when it's not easy.
Support	Family Support	Young people feel loved and supported in their family.
Support	Caring School Climate	Young people feel that their school supports them, encourages them, and cares about them.

POSITIVE FAMILY COMMUNICATION

When a young person is being bullied, **it's especially important to provide an atmosphere in which he or she can feel free to talk openly and honestly.** Your child may be ashamed of the events taking place. Knowing he or she has an open door to talk to you helps keep this matter from becoming a painful secret. Be available whenever and wherever your child wants to talk. If you're in the middle of something, arrange to talk as soon as possible.

If you suspect something is going on, but your adolescent isn't talking about it, ask questions. Do you feel safe at school? On the school bus? (If the answer is no, find out why.) Are you having trouble with another student or group of students? (If the answer is yes, follow up immediately.) Make it clear that you support your child completely.

Ask questions and listen to answers with an open mind and a focus on understanding. The more you know about your child's life, the more likely you are to know if he or she is a bully or is being bullied.

SAFETY

If your child does come to you about being bullied, **respond in a loving and accepting way.** Give your full attention to the entire story, and acknowledge how difficult and frightening the situation must be for him or her. Assure your child that her or his safety is extremely important to you and you will do everything you can to ensure it. Ask your child what he or she thinks should be done about the situation. You might also encourage her or him to talk with a teacher, friend, or guidance counselor for additional support.

Report the situation to the school immediately, and talk to your child's teachers, guidance counselor, and school administration about dealing with the problem. Continue to ask your child every day what is going on at school. This gives you the opportunity to keep up to date on the situation and know if things are getting better. Help your child understand that the behavior is the bully's problem and is not your child's fault.

RESISTANCE SKILLS

Teaching your adolescent **some basic resistance skills can help deflect the bullying situation.** Here are some tips to pass on to your child:

- Avoid or ignore the bully.

- Stay in groups when possible. Bullying is less likely to occur if your child is with friends.

- Say no to a bully's demands from the start. (Unless there's a weapon involved. In this case, a young person should give in to the demands and then tell an adult or call the police about the situation as soon as possible.)

- Help your child practice what to say to a bully. Practice assertive responses such as "Get lost—leave me alone" and "I don't like what you're doing."

- Don't fight back. Physical confrontation leads to increased victimization.

- Be confident. Use strong body language—walk tall, with head up high and back straight.

- Use humor. If your child can laugh at herself or himself, it doesn't give the bully the response he or she is looking for.

- If in danger, walk or run away.

SELF-ESTEEM

Now it's more important than ever to boost your child's self-esteem. If your child is being bullied, **assure her or him that the bullying is not her or his fault.** Remind your child how great he or she is. You could write Post-it notes of specific things you like about your child and leave them in hidden places around her or his room. Be sure to express your love regularly and often. Encourage your child to keep a journal of accomplishments. This can become a reference source of positive feelings. If you think your child's self-esteem is badly damaged, get professional help.

CARING

Bullying is a sign of emotional distress and can lead to serious problems if not dealt with. **If your child is the bully, you need to get help right away.** Seek the help of your child's doctor, teacher, principal, or school counselor. You may have to get help from a psychiatric professional if the bullying continues.

If your adolescent is bullying others, you can **establish an atmosphere of mutual caring and helpfulness within your home.** Set clear boundaries and expectations about how people should treat each other. Model respectful behavior. Show care and concern for neighbors. For example, are there elderly neighbors who need help with grocery shopping and house cleaning? If so, get your child involved. Teach your child nonviolent conflict resolution skills. You can find many books at the library on the subject, as well as sites on the Internet.

RESPONSIBILITY

 If your child is the bully in a situation, it's important that he or she take responsibility for those actions and for their consequences. Some good questions to ask bullies include:

- What did you do?

- Why was that a bad thing to do?

- Whom did you hurt?

- What were you trying to accomplish?

- Next time you have that goal, how will you meet it without causing any harm?

Support teachers and principals in school discipline action taken. If your child has agreed to any reciprocity, help her or him out by making sure there are no barriers to complete reciprocity.

HONESTY

 If your child is a bully, it is helpful to promote honesty in your family. Model honesty regularly. Be truthful with not only your family and friends but also with telemarketers and salespeople. If you find yourself fudging the truth, admit it and apologize. As a family, talk about situations at school and at work in which people acted honestly and dishonestly. Help your children talk through situations where it is tempting to be dishonest.

FAMILY SUPPORT

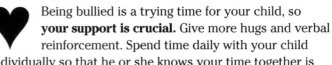 Being bullied is a trying time for your child, so **your support is crucial.** Give more hugs and verbal reinforcement. Spend time daily with your child individually so that he or she knows your time together is important.

If you have discovered that your child is a bully, accompany her or him to programs for adolescents and their families that deal with this issue.

CARING SCHOOL CLIMATE

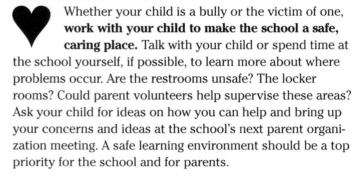 Whether your child is a bully or the victim of one, **work with your child to make the school a safe, caring place.** Talk with your child or spend time at the school yourself, if possible, to learn more about where problems occur. Are the restrooms unsafe? The locker rooms? Could parent volunteers help supervise these areas? Ask your child for ideas on how you can help and bring up your concerns and ideas at the school's next parent organization meeting. A safe learning environment should be a top priority for the school and for parents.

POSITIVE PEER RELATIONSHIPS

Bullying is a serious matter. It can make the victim's life miserable, and for the bully, it can mean serious consequences. But with the proper attention and support, it can be handled so young people can lead a normal daily life wherein they don't fear getting out of bed and going to school.

School Violence

Your Dilemma:

"Raj said a student hit a teacher with a chair at school today."

or

"Antoine came home very upset. He overheard two students threatening to hurt another kid. They told Rachel she'd 'better watch out.'"

ACTION TIPS

◆ Make sure your home has an atmosphere of openness and honesty. It's important that children feel they can tell you anything that's upsetting them.

◆ Encourage your children to become friends with other adults in whom they can confide when needed.

◆ Spend some time regularly with your children. This lets them know they are special and important.

◆ If you keep guns in your home, take precautions to safeguard your children.

◆ Work with school officials to come up with reasonable and safe guidelines for handling school violence in your community.

◆ Encourage young people to take on active roles in their school. Suggest organizing a peace rally or joining a peer mediation team.

◆ Be a model for positive conflict resolution. Learn how to settle your own disputes calmly and peacefully.

◆ Get your children involved in other activities besides watching TV. Encourage them to try music, theater, art classes, sports, clubs, community organizations, or congregational activities.

FACT: In the United States, more than 50 percent of all students
know of someone who has brought a weapon to school.

From: The Speak Up Campaign

School violence isn't new. But major events and the media give this issue a lot more attention now. The contributing factors to school violence are many. Negative peer pressure, gangs, cliques, isolation, alienation, crowding in schools, easy access to guns, violence in the home, the effects of alcohol and other drugs, violence in the media—these can all play a role.

Fears about safety in school affect young people in various ways. It certainly affects their ability to concentrate on schoolwork and to learn. They may skip school to avoid what frightens them, or they may bring their own weapons to school for protection. And teachers are affected, too. Instead of their focus being on helping students learn, they may end up spending a lot of time and energy on discipline or on trying to main-tain a safe environment in their classroom and the rest of the school.

The developmental assets are positive quali-ties, experiences, and skills that children need to grow up healthy and responsible. Parents, grand-parents, stepparents, or any other guardian of a child can use these assets as a framework to help them think through the new experiences they're encountering with their children. When dealing with the issue of school violence, the assets and larger asset categories you may want to consider looking at for guidance are Positive Family Communication, Other Adult Relationships, Bonding to School, Family Support, Safety, Parent Involvement in Schooling, Caring School Climate, Adult Role Models, and Constructive Use of Time.

ASSET TYPE	ASSET NAME	ASSET DESCRIPTION
Support	Positive Family Communication	Young people turn to their parents for advice and support. They have frequent, in-depth conversations with each other on a variety of topics. Parents are approachable and available when their children want to talk.
Support	Other Adult Relationships	Young people know other adults besides their parents they can turn to for advice and support. They have frequent, in-depth conversations with them. Ideally, three or more adults play this role in their lives.
Commitment to Learning	Bonding to School	Young people care about their school.
Support	Family Support	Young people feel loved and supported in their family.
Empowerment	Safety	Young people feel safe at home, at school, and in their neighborhood.
Support	Caring School Climate	Young people feel that their school supports them, encourages them, and cares about them.

(continued)

ASSET TYPE	ASSET NAME	ASSET DESCRIPTION
Boundaries and Expectations	Adult Role Models	Parents and other adults model positive, responsible behavior.
Constructive Use of Time	Asset #17 Creative Activities Asset #18 Youth Programs Asset #19 Religious Community Asset #20 Time at Home	Young people need constructive, enriching opportunities for growth through creative activities, youth programs, congregational involvement, and quality time at home.

POSITIVE FAMILY COMMUNICATION AND OTHER ADULT RELATIONSHIPS

One of the most important aspects of heading off school violence is for young people to feel that **they have adults they can go to for completely confidential communication.** This is crucial whether the adults are parents, teachers, guidance counselors, or coaches. In a society wherein we are told not to be snitches, it is important to let young people know that honesty and openness is a responsibility when it comes to the possibility of violence.

When your children want to talk, be available and really listen. **Help your children come up with solutions that fit the circumstances.** If your children are threatened or have heard of a threat, report it to school officials and law enforcement immediately. Or, call the Speak Up Campaign hot line at 1 (866) SPEAK UP. This nationwide number allows students to anonymously report weapon-related threats at their school.

BONDING TO SCHOOL

Recent research suggests that school shootings are related mostly to young people feeling disconnected from their schools. **Encourage young people to take activist roles in their own schools.** They might start by simply introducing themselves to one student they don't know every week. They can ask the school newspaper to write stories on conflict resolution and violence prevention in their school. They might set up an anonymous hot line where students can share concerns about school violence. They can join a peer mediation group at school or start such a program, hold a peace rally, or help the school set up a Web page devoted to school violence concerns and peacemaking.

FAMILY SUPPORT

Spending time with your children gives them a feeling of importance and self-worth. Children who truly feel good about themselves are less likely to act out in a violent way. Give more hugs and verbal rein-

forcement. Take at least 10 minutes every day to spend quality time with each of your children individually. When you choose to do family activities together that involve TV, film, or video games, choose nonviolent ones and discuss why you are choosing these.

SAFETY

Young people need to know that adults are doing everything possible to ensure their safety, and safety around the home is no different. **If you keep guns in your home, take precautions.** Lock them up and keep the key hidden. Use trigger guards on each weapon, and store ammunition separately from firearms. Urge your children to tell you if they know someone is carrying a weapon or if there is access to guns at a friend's house. If a number of young people live in your neighborhood, encourage your child to connect with them and their parents and talk about how to keep the school community safe.

Pay attention to what's going on in your child's life, and be alert to distress signals. Dramatic changes in attire, mood swings, or problems with friendships may be signs of trouble. A child who is overly withdrawn or preoccupied with violence needs attention and help. **Be alert to such signals not only in your own child but also in her or his friends.** Ask questions about what's going on at school, and make sure you're comfortable with the level of security that exists there.

PARENT INVOLVEMENT IN SCHOOLING

Parents can take an active role in how schools prepare for and deal with school violence. Ask school officials questions, such as what their plan is if they need to get in touch with a parent who cannot be reached. Support your child's school or district in efforts to get crisis training *before* a crisis. **Work with school officials to influence school policies** on violence, weapons, and school visitors. Pursue helping school administrators in developing plans to create processes and procedures to address the needs of students, staff, and parents in the aftermath of a critical event.

CARING SCHOOL CLIMATE

 Creating a safe environment for young people is the responsibility of everyone who's involved in educating them. **Get involved in your children's school's parent organization,** and help make the school a safe place for all children. Encourage your children to build relationships with teachers and students. The more connected the community, the safer it is.

ADULT ROLE MODELS

 Young people learn by watching the adults around them. **Show your children positive ways to manage conflict.** When in disagreements, communicate calmly and act peacefully. There are many good books and Internet sites on conflict resolution and peacemaking. Check out some of these with your children.

CONSTRUCTIVE USE OF TIME

 The media is one of the contributing factors to school violence and skews our perception of it. The American Academy of Pediatrics suggests that parents limit the amount of TV that children watch. They recommend only one to two hours per day. It's also important to guide your children away from violent video games, especially those that encourage shooting with guns. **There are a variety of ways to get your children away from TV and video games.** Encourage them to get involved in music, theater, or other arts. Help them find sports, clubs, or organizations at school or in the community that they enjoy. If you belong to a congregation, find activities in which your children can become involved there. Volunteer as a family for an organization that helps others.

A SAFER PLACE

Schools should be a place of learning, not a place of fear. We can help make our schools safer places for our children by getting involved in their schools and encouraging our children to get involved. But most of all, we need to pay attention and keep the lines of communication open with the young people in our lives, so they can come to us when they need to—so they know there is always some place safe.

Spotting the Warning Signs
That May Lead to School Violence

Part of positive family communication (asset #2) is talking with your children about the warning signs other students display if they have the potential to cause school violence. You may want to discuss the following list with your children. Explain that just because a person does these things does not mean he or she will automatically hurt another person, but these are simply some factors that have been recognized in people who have committed violent acts.

Be concerned if a student . . .

- plays with weapons of any kind;

- brags about acts of violence he or she would like to commit;

- repeatedly watches violent programs or plays violent video games;

- bullies or threatens other people;

- acts cruelly to pets or other animals;

- has talked to others about problems being bullied and feels isolated, angry, depressed, and frustrated by the situation;

- destroys property out of anger;

- has previously been truant, suspended, or expelled from school;

- has few or no close friends;

- has a serious history of disciplinary problems in the school and community;

- commits thefts or vandalism;

- expresses racist attitudes;

- is intolerant of others; and/or

- is in a gang or deals drugs.

If your child or someone he or she knows shows a number of these warning signs, seek help immediately. Tell a guidance counselor or school official. Seek counseling for these young people. If necessary, call the police.

Friends

Your Dilemma:

"De'Shawn is hanging out with a new crowd we're not so sure we can trust. He's come home late a few nights, and he doesn't always tell us where he's going anymore."

or

"Danielle just got in a huge fight with her friend Nancy. We really like Nancy. We'd like to see the two of them work things out."

ACTION TIPS

◆ Get to know your children's friends and their friends' parents or guardians, if possible. Make your home a welcoming place for your children and their friends.

◆ Help your adolescents learn how to resolve conflicts peacefully. Teach them a "feelings vocabulary" so they know how to express their emotions directly and constructively. Read about techniques for conflict resolution and share what you learn with your children.

◆ Work on developing interpersonal skills with your child.

◆ As much as you can, make positive comments about your children's friends. If you're concerned that a certain friend is a negative influence, it's time for an honest discussion in which you and your child listen and compromise.

◆ Let your children see how much you value your own friendships. Create opportunities for your children and your friends to interact. Demonstrate the give and take of friendship by modeling how friends help each other and work through problems together.

WHAT YOUNG PEOPLE SAY: "I like having all different kinds of friends—male and female, different religions, different races—because I can learn other ideas about life from them."

Adolescence may seem to bring a big change when it comes to friends. When they were 3 or 4, you were without question, the center of your children's world. But now that they're older their world has expanded, and the center of it has shifted out into their peer group. No matter how the situation may appear, they really do want us in their lives, but the people who seem to matter most now appear to be their friends.

This, of course, is understandable. Friendship is one of life's great blessings, something we hope our children will have in abundance. Through friendships, they are learning valuable social skills that will serve them well throughout their lives. But helping them navigate the swirling waters of the adolescent social scene can be a tricky business, one that requires both generosity and restraint. How can we offer our guidance and support without interfering?

The developmental assets are positive qualities, experiences, and skills that children need to grow up healthy and responsible. Parents, grandparents, stepparents, or any other guardian of a child can use these assets as a framework to help them think through the new experiences they're encountering with their children. When dealing with the issue of friends with your children, the assets you may want to consider looking at for guidance are Family Support, Interpersonal Competence, Peaceful Conflict Resolution, Positive Peer Influence, and Adult Role Models.

ASSET TYPE	ASSET NAME	ASSET DESCRIPTION
Support	Family Support	Young people feel loved and supported in their family.
Social Competencies	Interpersonal Competence	Young people have empathy, sensitivity, and friendship skills.
Social Competencies	Peaceful Conflict Resolution	Young people seek to resolve conflicts nonviolently.
Boundaries and Expectations	Positive Peer Influence	Young people's best friends model responsible behavior. They are a good influence. They do well at school and stay away from risky behaviors such as alcohol and other drug use.
Boundaries and Expectations	Adult Role Models	Parents and other adults model positive, responsible behavior.

FAMILY SUPPORT

 One way to offer guidance and support is to **make your home a welcoming place for all young people.** This is important for a number of reasons. It communicates to all of the adolescents who come there that they are valued. It provides them with a safe and healthy place to hang out. And it makes it more likely that your own children will spend time at home, so you know where they are. Making your home comfortable for young people has less to do with the physical space than with the emotional atmosphere. If you're genuinely glad they're there—and communicate this through your speech, body language, and actions—they should feel welcome and at ease.

Get to know your child's friends. Spend time with them, engage them in conversation, learn about their interests. Respect their need for privacy, of course, but make the effort to find out what's going on in their lives. Most young people are happy to talk with friends' parents. Some caregivers have noticed that young people who aren't interested in talking with them are actually disengaged from adults in general, and this was a red flag that helped them stay alert to risky behavior.

Food is always a good icebreaker. Invite your child and her or his friends to bake cookies or bread with you or join you to pop popcorn. Or, see if they'd be interested in learning how to cook a favorite meal. Such activities provide opportunities for relaxed conversations in which even shy adolescents can start to feel more comfortable. You might **also include them in other activities,** such as art projects, gardening, or washing the car. Or, invite them over to watch a movie with your family and then talk about the film together afterwards.

Get to know the parents or guardian of your children's friends, too. Invite them to dinner, or have a party for the caregivers of all the young people in your children's group of friends. Share your thoughts about creating a supportive environment for the children. Discuss any concerns you have about what's going on in the group. And agree to keep each other informed about where the young people are and what they're doing.

Know that **it is natural for some young people to have one or two close friends rather than many friends.** Research suggests that one good friend is all that is important. Some young people may have a shy personality, influenced by temperament and their early experiences. If you're bothered that your child doesn't have more friends, you may want to reflect on why your child's introversion bothers you.

INTERPERSONAL COMPETENCE

 Making and keeping friends may come more naturally to some young people than others. **You can help your child build her or his "people" skills.** Practice interpersonal skills together, such as meeting people, starting conversations, asking questions, and finding similar interests. Invite over dinner guests and, as a family, spend time talking with your guests. Model empathy and sensitivity with your child, and discuss why these are important interpersonal skills.

Be intentional about helping your child learn about friendships and interacting with others. Here are a few ideas:

- Let your child grieve when a relationship sours or fades.
- Introduce your child to people of many different ages.
- Start conversations with your child about relationships.

PEACEFUL CONFLICT RESOLUTION

One of the most difficult and painful aspects of young people's friendships is how fickle the social scene can be. Your child may be in with a popular crowd one week and out in the cold the next. Or, he or she may be inseparable from a certain friend or two for a long stretch, only to have those relationships collapse into bitter disputes. Suddenly it's as if "Everyone hates me," and life is steeped in misery.

The volatility of relationships during the adolescent years can be nearly as painful to watch as to experience firsthand. We may be tempted to jump in and try to help "fix" the situation, and in extreme circumstances (for example, if your child is the target of a bully) this may be appropriate. For the most part, however, we have to content ourselves with watching from the sidelines and trying to supply the moral support that will help them get through the hard times. Much as we want to protect them from suffering, young people have to learn about the hardships of human relationships on their own. Make sure you are a kind of safety net for your children during such rough times.

We can, however, teach them about resolving conflicts peacefully. We can **help them develop a "feelings vocabulary"** so they know how to express their emotions directly. And we can **teach them how to use "I" statements,** such as "I feel angry when you do that" instead of "You make me so mad." Learning to phrase things in terms of your own feelings is an important part of learning to take responsibility for your own emotions. The guidance counselor or librarian at your adolescent's school may be able to recommend books on peaceful conflict resolution that your family could read together and discuss.

POSITIVE PEER INFLUENCE

Inevitably, we will like some of our children's friends more than others. At times, this can pose a real dilemma, especially if we suspect that certain friends are making unhealthy choices, such as using drugs or engaging in sex. On the one hand, if we don't say anything, we worry. On the other hand, if we do say something, we risk prompting our children to defend the friendship, thereby making them even more determined to maintain it.

As much as possible, **try to keep your remarks about your children's friends upbeat and friendly.** Without going overboard, affirm the friendships you regard as positive. (For example, you might tell them how much you enjoy a particular friend.) At the same time, make an effort to reach out to the friends you find less appealing. You may find that your own biases (for example, about their style of dress or social skills) kept you from seeing their positive traits. You and your family may also be able to exert a positive influence on them, bringing them more into your child's orbit than the other way around.

If that doesn't work and you're concerned that the situation is really getting out of hand with a particular friend or group of friends, it's time for a frank discussion. **Express your concerns calmly and openly, and listen closely to what your child has to say about the matter.** Try to find some grounds for agreement about how to handle the situation, and then set some clear limits. For example, you might say "Arthur is welcome here anytime, but I don't want you

driving with him." Or, "You can get together with Steph after school twice a week, but not every day."

ADULT ROLE MODELS

Having healthy friendships of our own is a tremendous resource for parents and guardians. Not only can our friends support and encourage us through the challenges of raising children, but also they can help us model for our children how to create balanced relationships in their own lives. **It's important for young people to see that we place a high value on friendship and that we invest time and energy in maintaining our connections with friends.** It can also be helpful for them to see that we can ask our friends for help, work through problems in our friendships, set boundaries on relationships that are draining, and find ways for our friends and family to spend meaningful time together.

LIFELONG COMPANIONS

The ability to form deep and lasting friendships is an important life skill and one that adolescents work hard at acquiring. It's not an easy task, set amid the bumpy terrain of adolescence and filled with all the drama of the human condition. And our role is necessarily limited; there is much about friendship that our children simply have to work out for themselves.

But we can give them our support. To succeed—to learn how to be a good friend and to have good friends—they need to respect and care for themselves and for others, and that's where we can help them. We can make our homes welcoming, encourage them through the rough spots, listen to their woes, set meaningful boundaries, and celebrate friendship in our own lives. In these ways, we can help them sow the seeds of a life rich with friends.

Talking about Friends

Here are some questions that can get a discussion about friends going with your children:

- What do you value in your closest friends?

- What do your friends value in you?

- Is it easy for you to make friends? If not, what seems to make it difficult?

- Is it easy for you to keep friendships going? If not, what seems to cause problems?

- Do you have friends of different ages? Races? Religions? Ethnic backgrounds? Genders?

- What is difficult or easy in having a friendship with a person from a different gender or the same gender?

- What are some things you and your friends have in common?

- What are some things you don't have in common with your friends?

- What have you learned through your friendships?

- What advice would you give to someone who has a hard time making friends?

- How have your friendships changed over the years?

- Have you ever felt rejected by a friend? If you have, how did you handle the rejection? Do you still think about it?

- Do you develop close friendships quickly and easily, or are you hesitant to get involved in a close friendship?

Other Caring, Responsible Adults

Your Dilemma:

"Sometimes I don't feel like we're enough. We wish Kai had some other adults to talk with."

or

"I don't know if Julie has any role models in her life besides singers and actresses."

ACTION TIPS

◆ Talk to your children about the value of friendship and about caring adults they might be interested in getting to know better.

◆ Get to know your neighbors, and encourage your children to do the same. The effort you put into creating a caring atmosphere in your neighborhood will help make it a stronger, more vibrant community and will benefit everyone who lives there.

◆ Encourage your child to get involved in youth programs that are supervised by caring adults, such as supportive coaches, instructors, or youth group leaders.

◆ Talk to people at your child's school and at your place of worship to see if there are adults who have an interest in common with your child. See if they might be available to spend time with your son or daughter.

◆ Keep safety in mind when bringing new adults into your child's life.

◆ Connect your child with other adults who share her or his interests. This is one way you don't have to do activities you don't like or do well, and your child can still share them with someone special.

◆ Point out to your child that research shows that teens who have several caring adults in their lives are more likely to succeed and feel good about themselves.

FACT: In 2002, a poll of parents in the United States showed that despite feelings of success, most parents received little support or affirmation for their parenting efforts.

From: *Building Strong Families* a report by YMCA and Search Institute

In many cultures, communities, and individual families, children have close, nurturing relationships with a number of adults—aunts, uncles, grandparents, neighbors, and other respected elders in the community. These caring adults help to teach, guide, and even discipline young people. Parents are no less important because of this extended family; they simply have the support of others who care about their children. They don't have to do everything themselves.

For others, though, families are separate, somewhat lonely units, with relatively little support from other sources. Yet imagine how much richer children's lives might be if there were other trusted adults to whom they could turn for support and encouragement. And what a relief for parents or guardians to know that other people can provide some of what their adolescents need.

We may not be able to create an entire extended family for them, but if we can help our children establish two or three friendships with other caring adults, we can be sure that their lives—and our own—will be that much richer.

The developmental assets are positive qualities, experiences, and skills that children need to grow up healthy and responsible. Parents, grandparents, stepparents, or any other guardian of a child can use these assets as a framework to help them think through the new experiences they're encountering with their children. When dealing with the issue of other caring adults and your family, the assets you may want to consider looking at for guidance are Positive Family Communication, Caring Neighborhood, Caring School Climate, Safety, Youth Programs, and Religious Community.

ASSET TYPE	ASSET NAME	ASSET DESCRIPTION
Support	Positive Family Communication	Young people turn to their parents for advice and support. They have frequent, in-depth conversations with each other on a variety of topics. Parents are approachable and available when their children want to talk.
Support	Caring Neighborhood	Young people feel that their neighbors support them, encourage them, and care about them.
Support	Caring School Climate	Young people feel that their school supports them, encourages them, and cares about them.
Empowerment	Safety	Young people feel safe at home, at school, and in their neighborhood.
Constructive Use of Time	Youth Programs	Young people spend three or more hours each week in sports, clubs, or organizations at school and/or in the community.
Constructive Use of Time	Religious Community	Young people spend one or more hours each week in religious services or participating in spiritual activities.

POSITIVE FAMILY COMMUNICATION

Spend time as a family talking about the importance of friendship in our lives. Find out whether your children consider friendship with adults to be valuable or even possible. Ask them why or why not. See if there are adults they might want to get to know better, and discuss how to go about establishing a friendship with them. Offer your support in talking to these adults if your child feels that would be helpful. For example, suggest inviting the adult over for dinner sometime so everyone can talk together.

Make a list together of the adults your child has regular contact with, such as teachers, coaches, neighbors, bus drivers, and employers. **Write a short note to one or more of these people, thanking them for their interest in and concern for your child.**

CARING NEIGHBORHOOD

Ideally, a neighborhood is a place where everyone feels safe, comfortable, and valued, and where young people and adults treat each other with generosity and respect. Neighbors watch out for each other, respect each other, and give each other a hand whenever possible.

Unfortunately, many neighborhoods don't work that way. Many of us don't even know our neighbors, so we miss out on having people nearby who care about us—and our children miss out, too. But even if you wouldn't currently describe where you live as a "caring neighborhood," you can do a lot to improve the situation.

Get to know your neighbors. Invite them to dinner and spend time as a family talking with them. Help your children learn to "build bridges" of shared interests with other people. If you have neighbors or friends who have a hobby or interest in common with your child, ask them if they'd be willing to meet with your child to talk about it.

Encourage your children to make a habit of helping people around the neighborhood, without expecting payment. Offering to walk someone's dog or rake someone's yard is a great way to establish a friendly and caring atmosphere in the neighborhood.

CARING SCHOOL CLIMATE

See if a mentoring program is available through your child's school or another community organization. If so, find out about it and see if your child would like to join. If no such program is available, talk to teachers, administrators, and other parents about starting one. Talk to other parents about whether their adolescent children have adult friends and how these friendships began.

SAFETY

You do need to be cautious about the adults with whom your child spends time. You want your child to be with a responsible, caring adult, not someone who is going to harm them in some way. It's best to try to get to know a new person in a group setting first if possible. Unless you are completely confident in this new person in your child's life, you will want other people to be around when they are spending time together. As the relationship begins, be alert to signs of any inappropriate behavior.

YOUTH PROGRAMS

Learn about events and programs in your community that offer young people the opportunity to meet caring adults. Possibilities include:

- Activities at the local YWCA, YMCA, Boys and Girls Club, 4H, or community center;
- Art, drama, or music classes;
- Camp Fire USA, Scouts, or other troops;
- Organized athletics; and/or
- Summer camps focused on a specific area of interest (such as horseback riding or chess).

RELIGIOUS COMMUNITY

Reach out to people in your congregation who have shown interest in your child. See if there are trusted adults who might be available to spend time with your child regularly or if there are youth programs and activities in which your child can participate. Help educate other adults about the importance of valuing and supporting young people. Demonstrate what you would like for your child by being a mentor yourself.

CARING FRIENDSHIPS

Young people need to feel a strong connection with a number of caring adults. The role of mentor, coach, or guide doesn't replace the role of a child's parents or guardian but actually enhances it by creating a broader base of support for the child. Young people who know they have several trusted adult friends to talk to have a greater sense of belonging to a community of people who care about them.

Dating

Your Dilemma:

**"Gavin has mentioned a girl he's seeing.
We don't even know what she looks like."**
or
**"We're not fond of Jennifer's new boyfriend, Richard.
Should we say something?"**

ACTION TIPS

◆ Encourage open communication in your family. Whether talking about someone new they're seeing or the heartache of a breakup, young people need to know they have someone to turn to who will take their situation seriously.

◆ If you don't care for the people your children are dating, avoid making negative comments. Be sensitive yet honest if your children actually ask for your opinion. What you think and how you express it matters more than you may realize.

◆ Invite your children's dates to come to where you live for family meals and other activities. Get to know each other.

◆ As safety precautions, encourage your children to go on dates in groups and to take dates to public places.

◆ Decide how you feel about your children riding in cars with other young people, especially if the driver is very inexperienced.

◆ Discuss the boundaries and consequences of dating with your children. Agree on family guidelines.

◆ Keep children involved in after-school clubs and programs, sports, and community organizations.

◆ Encourage young people to maintain their other friendships while dating.

FACT: In one survey of teens aged 12 to 17, 55 percent said that adolescents should be allowed to begin steady dating at age 15 or younger.

From: National Campaign to Prevent Teen Pregnancy

Dating can be a major part of an adolescent's life. And it's a delicate matter to guide young people as they enter this world of mixed emotions, changing social demands, and strong physical impulses. We worry that they're too young, that their safety is at stake, that their hearts will be broken. During this emotional time, they need us more than ever. They need to know we're there and that we love them enough to set and maintain firm boundaries for them.

The developmental assets are positive qualities, experiences, and skills that children need to grow up healthy and responsible. Parents, grandparents, stepparents, or any other guardian of a child can use these assets as a framework to help them think through the new experiences they're encountering with their children. When dealing with the issue of your children dating, the assets and asset categories you may want to consider looking at for guidance are Family Boundaries, Constructive Use of Time, Positive Peer Influence, Family Support, Positive Family Communication, Interpersonal Competence, and Safety.

ASSET TYPE	ASSET NAME	ASSET DESCRIPTION
Boundaries and Expectations	Family Boundaries	Parents set clear rules and consequences for their children's behavior. They monitor their children's whereabouts.
Constructive Use of Time	Asset #17 Creative Activities Asset #18 Youth Programs Asset #19 Religious Community Asset #20 Time at Home	Young people need constructive, enriching opportunities for growth through creative activities, youth programs, congregational involvement, and quality time at home.
Boundaries and Expectations	Positive Peer Influence	Young people's best friends model responsible behavior. They are a good influence. They do well at school and stay away from risky behaviors such as alcohol and other drug use.
Support	Family Support	Young people feel loved and supported in their family.
Support	Positive Family Communication	Young people turn to their parents for advice and support. They have frequent, in-depth conversations with each other on a variety of topics. Parents are approachable and available when their children want to talk.
Social Competencies	Interpersonal Competence	Young people have empathy, sensitivity, and friendship skills.
Empowerment	Safety	Young people feel safe at home, at school, and in their neighborhood.

FAMILY BOUNDARIES

The big question in your family will probably be: When are our children ready to date? Of course, the answer can be different depending on individual parents and their children. Most youth younger than 14, however, do not have the social skills necessary to handle dating situations. In general, most girls begin dating about age 14 or 15, and most boys begin at about age 15 or 16. Young people likely feel romantic stirrings before they are ready for full-fledged dating. They may want to use the phone more for getting to know each other.

Before your children start dating, have clear boundaries in place, with specific consequences. This way, you don't have to embarrass your adolescents in front of their dates and say what is expected and what could happen if those expectations are not met. One boundary may be that the relationship is expected not to interfere with schoolwork or other activities and that it will still allow time for family and friends. Another boundary may be following the curfew you set. You can also set guidelines for where, when, and how often your children go out on dates. When they do go on a date, know where they're going and what they plan to do. Talk about these boundaries and expectations together, and meet regularly to make sure they are working. Discuss with your children any cultural community expectations and norms as well.

And then there's the topic of sex. This is the time to **share what values you have and why and how those relate to the boundaries you've set.** But your boundaries may not always be followed. Your adolescents need to know that if they do decide to engage in sex, they should talk with their partner first, discuss each other's sexual history, and take precautions to prevent disease and unplanned pregnancy. It's best if such frank advice can come from adults they trust—not peers who don't have complete information.

CONSTRUCTIVE USE OF TIME

The feeling of being with someone special can be easy to get caught up in for people of any age. But it can be especially overwhelming for adolescents. It's important for young people to maintain a balance between the time they spend with a boyfriend or girlfriend and the time they spend involved in other activities. **They should stay involved in after-school clubs or programs, sports, or community organizations.** All of these activities help contribute to who they are as individuals and help them stay resilient in the face of a breakup. Healthy relationships consist of people who are meeting their own needs for growth, not just meeting the needs of someone else. Help your children recognize this important distinction.

POSITIVE PEER INFLUENCE

Sometimes a dating relationship can become all-consuming for adolescents. Girls especially have a tendency to focus on their relationship and drop their peers. **It's important that children not lose touch with their other friends when dating.** During adolescence, dating relationships are often fleeting, and adolescents need the support of friends they can count on. Other friends help young people maintain their identity.

FAMILY SUPPORT

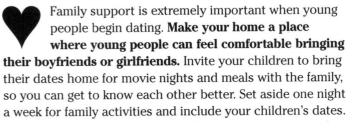

Family support is extremely important when young people begin dating. **Make your home a place where young people can feel comfortable bringing their boyfriends or girlfriends.** Invite your children to bring their dates home for movie nights and meals with the family, so you can get to know each other better. Set aside one night a week for family activities and include your children's dates.

Having a supportive family at home may take some of the sting out of a breakup. **Be sure your children know how much you love and appreciate them.** Be there to help your children talk about their painful feelings. Encourage them to start hanging out with friends again if they are closing themselves off from the outside world.

POSITIVE FAMILY COMMUNICATION

Dating can be a tricky topic of discussion; you want to let your children know you're interested in their lives, yet at the same time you don't want to be intrusive. **Encourage your children to talk about the people they're interested in.** You can make it easy for them by regularly and casually asking about what's going on in their lives. Remember specific names and events your children tell you about, and share your own memories of dating experiences. Make it clear that you're always available to talk.

Even if you dislike someone your son or daughter is dating, try to stay neutral. Avoid negative comments. These often encourage adolescents to continue a relationship of which they may actually be growing tired. If they ask what you think of the person, be honest but tactful.

Perhaps the most difficult part of young relationships is that they seldom last. Breakups happen for a variety of reasons: a person doesn't feel treated as an equal, a person feels pressured, a person feels abused, or a person simply loses interest. Whatever the reason, breaking up hurts—and can sometimes trigger a poor self-concept. Young people may react by behaving recklessly. **Be available to talk with your children** if they seem to need help sorting through difficult feelings.

Adolescence is a time of uncertainty, and even gentle,

well-intentioned comments can be taken the wrong way or cause insecurity. Therefore, **try to avoid teasing your children about dating.**

INTERPERSONAL COMPETENCE

 Healthy relationships can take work, even with the right partner. **Talk with your children about what traits make a good partner,** that there's more to a boyfriend or girlfriend than their just being cute. Discuss the qualities that make a dating relationship healthy, such as caring, communication, equality, respect, and trust.

SAFETY

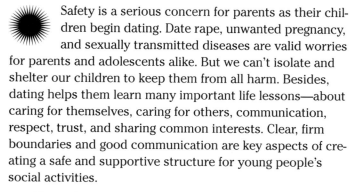 Safety is a serious concern for parents as their children begin dating. Date rape, unwanted pregnancy, and sexually transmitted diseases are valid worries for parents and adolescents alike. But we can't isolate and shelter our children to keep them from all harm. Besides, dating helps them learn many important life lessons—about caring for themselves, caring for others, communication, respect, trust, and sharing common interests. Clear, firm boundaries and good communication are key aspects of creating a safe and supportive structure for young people's social activities.

- **Always be sure you know where your children are going and with whom.** This may seem obvious, but it can be easy to assume that things are okay without checking it out. Be thorough. Call the parents or guardian of the girl whose party your child is going to, for example. Are they aware of the plan? Are they going to be present? Be sure all your questions are answered to your satisfaction before you consent.

- **Trust your instincts.** If something doesn't feel right, check it out. If you can't shake the feeling that something is wrong, you may well be right.

- **Talk with your children about the effects of alcohol and other drugs on people's judgment.** Emphasize the dangers of driving while intoxicated, and make it clear you expect them not to get in a car with someone who has been using alcohol or other drugs. Let them know that they can always call you if they need a ride home— no questions asked.

- **Make sure your children have the right information on unwanted pregnancy, date rape, and sexually transmitted diseases.** Provide information on these topics. Having the correct information may protect them from negative peer pressure.

- **Encourage group dating.** On group dates, adolescents are less likely to engage in sexual activity.

- **Tell your children to stay in public places when out on dates.** Parking in isolated spots is risky for all kinds of reasons. They can still have fun where other people are around.

- **Discuss how you feel about new situations and places,** such as riding in cars with inexperienced drivers and going to new dance clubs. You may or may not be comfortable with your children doing these things.

MAINTAINING BALANCE

Dating has many benefits. Through dating, young people build self-confidence and discover who they are. They learn social skills and how to develop a close relationship with another person. Parents' guidance can help adolescents keep dating in balance with the other aspects of their lives and help keep them safe, while still giving them room to explore and have fun.

Sexuality

Your Dilemma:

"Jamal is getting to that age where we think we need to talk to him more about sex, but we're nervous about discussing it."
or
"I think Mandy is sexually active. What should I do?"

ACTION TIPS

◆ Foster your children's self-esteem by treating them with respect and letting them know how much you love them. Young people who feel good about themselves are better able to resist peer pressure and take care of themselves.

◆ Set clear boundaries and let your children know what your expectations are about sexual conduct. Knowing what's expected is often a relief to young people.

◆ Monitor TV and Internet use to limit access to sexually explicit programs and sites.

◆ Help create safe forums for young people to talk about sex and other issues they're concerned about. See if a teacher or guidance counselor will offer an after-school discussion group.

◆ If you feel too uncomfortable talking about sex with your children, you could consider asking an extended family member to do it. You could also see if the Internet, your adolescent's school, other parents, or bookstores have advice, workbooks, etc. for helping you discuss this topic with your children.

WHAT YOUNG PEOPLE SAY: "Help us be responsible if we choose to be sexually active."

In a culture that uses sex to sell everything from beer to movies to pickup trucks, it's hard to help young people develop a healthy and appropriate attitude toward their own sexuality. Every day, we're bombarded with sexual imagery. Young people are confronted by an especially bewildering array of mixed messages about sexual behavior. Jerry Springer is not the person most of us would choose to educate our children about sex, but that's typical of the quality of information they often receive.

Despite its constant presence as an advertising tool and mode of entertainment, sex remains such an electrifying subject for many of us that we try to ignore it. We may vaguely tell our children what we think they need to know, and hope they'll leave it at that. We may even assume they understand more than they actually do.

Young people need clear and loving guidance in this part of their lives as much as—or possibly more than—any other. Our children are sexual beings, quickly maturing into adults capable of expressing their sexuality. We want to be sure they have the information, self-esteem, and restraint to make healthy and appropriate choices. They need more from us than simply to be told: "Just say no."

The developmental assets are positive qualities, experiences, and skills that children need to grow up healthy and responsible. Parents, grandparents, stepparents, or any other guardian of a child can use these assets as a framework to help them think through the new experiences they're encountering with their children. When your family is dealing with issues related to sexuality, the assets you may want to consider looking at for guidance are Self-Esteem, Positive Family Communication, High Expectations, Family Support, Family Boundaries, and Community Values Youth.

ASSET TYPE	ASSET NAME	ASSET DESCRIPTION
Positive Identity	Self-Esteem	Young people feel good about themselves.
Support	Positive Family Communication	Young people turn to their parents for advice and support. They have frequent, in-depth conversations with each other on a variety of topics. Parents are approachable and available when their children want to talk.
Boundaries and Expectations	High Expectations	Parents and teachers encourage young people to do well.
Support	Family Support	Young people feel loved and supported in their family.
Boundaries and Expectations	Family Boundaries	Parents set clear rules and consequences for their children's behavior. They monitor their children's whereabouts.
Empowerment	Community Values Youth	Young people perceive that adults in the community value them.

SELF-ESTEEM

The saying "Your body is a temple" may be old, but it retains an important kernel of truth. To have an attitude of respect and care for oneself is a great blessing, a solid foundation on which to build a happy and responsible life. Young people who believe in their own worth—who feel valued for who they are rather than what they do or who likes them—are in a much better position to make wise choices than those who do not. **Fostering adolescents' self-respect can take many forms:**

- Treat them with respect. Listen when they speak. Make the extra effort not to yell, even if you're angry.

- Tell them you love them—often—even if they make a show of being "too old for all that" or quickly brush it off.

- Be affectionate with your children and with your spouse or partner. By modeling a loving and respectful relationship, you give your children the opportunity to see that it's possible for them to create harmonious relationships in their own lives, even when two people may disagree at times.

- Celebrate their triumphs, and accept their failures with grace. Let them know you believe in them.

- Encourage them to take care of themselves before taking care of others.

POSITIVE FAMILY COMMUNICATION

Hopefully, you've started talking about sexuality with your child in appropriate ways at an early age. If sex hasn't really been a topic of discussion in your family, it can be difficult to broach the subject. A formal "Sex Talk," with a particular agenda and a long list of do's and don'ts, is unlikely to result in a candid discussion. **A less lengthy and more informal approach probably has a greater chance for success.** Start slowly and try to keep it light. Remember that humor is a great ally. It's good to have such a casual talk *before* any dilemma regarding sexuality comes up with your child.

You might pick a TV show or movie that deals with a specific sexual topic and talk about that. Ask if your children agree or disagree with the way the issue is presented, and share your own view. Discuss gender roles and their effects on people's self-esteem. For example, you might analyze the way women are portrayed in a sexually provocative magazine ad and discuss how this might affect the self-image of a young girl reading the magazine.

Discuss the different levels of expressing sexuality. Sexual intercourse is a big part of sexuality, but it isn't the only topic. Expressing affection, another form of sexuality, is

an area where you'll want to talk about setting boundaries.

Some parents may not be okay with public displays of affection, making out on the couch, or with a couple spending time in a bedroom behind closed doors. Some parents may decide the best option is to allow a couple some alone time in the family room but with doors open. Talk with your child about what boundaries you think are best and give your reasons why.

Be open and nonjudgmental in your discussions of sexual matters. Invite your children's questions, and encourage them to discuss their concerns. Encourage them to talk to other trusted adults as well. If you're uncomfortable with the whole topic—or a particular part of it—don't be afraid to say so. But let your children know that sexuality is an important part of life and that families need to learn how to talk about it together.

HIGH EXPECTATIONS

Having clear boundaries about sexual behavior may actually be a relief to young people. When they know what's expected, young people don't have to struggle as much with making all the decisions for themselves. You might, for example, simply tell your children you expect them not to have sex, drink alcohol, or use other drugs while they're adolescents. Explain why you believe this is important, and discuss your cultural community's expectations and values regarding these activities. Then encourage them to make a commitment to abstaining from such activities during their adolescent years. This way your children know exactly where the line is, and they don't have to try to figure it out on their own every time.

Even if you set clear boundaries, this doesn't necessarily mean your children will heed them. Restraint in sexual matters can be difficult at any age, but the surging hormones and limited impulse control of adolescence can make it especially challenging.

If you discover that your child has become or intends to become sexually active, do your best to receive this news with a measure of calm and compassion. Keep in mind that he or she may be experiencing a lot of different emotions, and that **the most helpful thing you can do is to keep the lines of communication open.** Make it clear that you're unhappy with the *choices,* not with the child. **Your love and acceptance are more important than ever.** Rather than taking a punitive approach, offer your support and encouragement in making wiser choices in the future. Remind your child again about safety from disease and preventing pregnancy. Make yourself available to talk. Try spending time together doing simple activities, such as gardening or washing the car, which will allow natural conversations to arise.

FAMILY SUPPORT

An adolescent who is gay or bisexual is likely to need extra help in coming to terms with her or his sexuality. The pressures of coping with homophobic cultural norms can be especially intense for young people, and their fear of rejection may be strong. "Coming out" requires a tremendous amount of courage. Meeting this courage and vulnerability with an open and generous heart is a powerful act of love.

Accepting a child's homosexuality may be difficult for some parents. If this is true for you, it's important to seek help and guidance. Sometimes a parent's response is: What will people think of me? more than their response is: What will people think of my child? **Understanding your own fears and judgments will help you gain access to the supply of unconditional love you have for your child.** If you feel you need support for yourself or your adolescent during this time, don't be afraid to seek another caring, trustworthy adult who can be there for you and your child.

Clear boundaries and high expectations are as important for gay or bisexual adolescents as for heterosexual youth. **Let your children know what you expect of them and why.** Frank discussions are essential to creating an atmosphere in which understanding can grow and your children's self-esteem can flourish.

Establishing intimate relationships cross-racially or cross-culturally may cause tension within some families and cultural communities. Explain whatever concerns you may have to your children as well as the impact such relationships may have on the family and the community. In the end, the choice will be up to your children. **It's important to let them know that you will continue to love them no matter what they choose in a relationship.**

FAMILY BOUNDARIES

Television and the Internet are filled with sexual content, and young people who have unlimited access to these media may tend to gravitate to sexually explicit programs and sites. **It's important to monitor the *source* of sexual information young people are getting,** not to keep them in the dark, but rather to be sure they get appropriate and helpful information.

Be aware of the content of programs your children watch and sites they visit. If they seem particularly drawn to sexually explicit material, **offer them appropriate books and** other materials that can satisfy their natural curiosity in a healthy way. Or, direct them to people who can offer good information, such as a family doctor or sex education teacher.

Be sure that physical activity is part of your children's lives. Whether it's dance, athletics, or skating at the park, exercise not only has countless physical benefits, it's a great way to express the body's natural exuberance. Having an outlet for all that youthful energy can help young people feel more at ease with themselves.

COMMUNITY VALUES YOUTH

Our schools and communities can and should support young people in developing healthy self-esteem and in making wise choices. We can help them by:

- **Voicing opposition to sexually suggestive advertising aimed at young people** and sexually provocative or exploitive ads that use young people to sell products.

- **Working with others in the community** to reduce adolescents' access to sexually explicit materials.

- **Creating safe opportunities for young people to learn about and discuss sexuality and other issues of concern to them.** For example, maybe a school guidance counselor or nurse would be willing to run an after-school discussion group. Or, a local clinic could sponsor a forum with input from health professionals.

- **Providing youth groups within our congregations** to help young people learn restraint and give them the opportunity to support and encourage each other in making good choices.

THE ANCIENT DANCE

Every culture has rites and customs that govern sexual interaction, and learning responsible sexual behavior is an important part of becoming an adult. Unfortunately, in our culture, sex is often a marketing tool, robbing it of much of the reverence—and the playfulness—with which it deserves to be treated. This dehumanizing trend is especially damaging for young people. We need to create safe, appropriate ways for young people to celebrate their aliveness and natural desires. In so doing, we teach them to become responsible and aware men and women. And we give them the help and guidance they need as they learn their part in the dance of life.

Stress Management

Your Dilemma:

**"Nicholas has to give an oral report tomorrow, and he's really
stressed out. I don't know how to help him calm down."**

or

**"Talisha has been having trouble sleeping.
I think something is bothering her."**

ACTION TIPS

◆ Help young people regain their sense of control and personal power by sharing relaxation techniques with them. You might try teaching your children breathing exercises or learning meditation techniques together.

◆ Pay attention to signs of stress in your children. When they want to talk, be available to listen and give support and affection.

◆ Encourage your children to go to the source of stress when a specific relationship is the cause. Sometimes a reasonable conversation can work wonders.

◆ Talk openly about upcoming changes, and ask your children about changes that are occurring in their lives.

◆ Model a lifestyle that's as stress-free as possible—make an effort to eat well, get plenty of rest, and make time for your family.

◆ Help your adolescent learn that it's okay to say no—that having too much to do can be overwhelming.

◆ Encourage your children to plan ahead for their day's activities. To-do lists and daily goals can help give a feeling of organization and control.

FACT: Many scientists and health professionals agree that stress is a factor in more than 80 percent of illness, physical dysfunction, and pain.

From: *Emotional Health*, Iowa Public Television

Stress is a serious problem for nearly everyone in our society—and not just adults. The carefree days of youth are really a myth. For some young people, there's school, work, sports, and homework, just for starters. That's not counting various pressures from family and peers to succeed, to fit in, to care for brothers and sisters, and to make decisions about the future. That's a lot to have on your mind. For many others, there's boredom, which brings its own form of stress.

A little stress can be good; it keeps us alert and on our toes. But too much stress is harmful—whether it's short-term or whether it hangs around, causing long-term problems. Young people suffering from too much stress may be irritable and may not get along well with others. They may have difficulty concentrating on important matters like school and work. They may not be able to sleep. Their appetite may disappear, or they may overeat.

Young people who don't know how to handle stress may feel like their world is falling apart. They may not know where to turn or how to start making things better. For that matter, they may not even realize they are under stress. That's where we can help.

The developmental assets are positive qualities, experiences, and skills that children need to grow up healthy and responsible. Parents, grandparents, stepparents, or any other guardian of a child can use these assets as a framework to help them think through the new experiences they're encountering with their children. When trying to help your children deal with stress, the assets you may want to consider looking at for guidance are Personal Power, Positive Family Communication, Adult Role Models, Resistance Skills, and Planning and Decision Making.

ASSET TYPE	ASSET NAME	ASSET DESCRIPTION
Positive Identity	Personal Power	Young people feel that they have control over many things that happen to them.
Support	Positive Family Communication	Young people turn to their parents for advice and support. They have frequent, in-depth conversations with each other on a variety of topics. Parents are approachable and available when their children want to talk.
Boundaries and Expectations	Adult Role Models	Parents and other adults model positive, responsible behavior.
Social Competencies	Resistance Skills	Young people can resist negative peer pressure and avoid dangerous situations.
Social Competencies	Planning and Decision Making	Young people know how to plan ahead and make choices.

ONAL POWER

One of the main aspects of stress is that we feel a loss of control. **It's important to help young people regain their feeling of power. You can do this by teaching them relaxation techniques.** Try a deep-breathing exercise in which you inhale for a slow count of six, hold the breath for a count of four, and then release the breath over a count of six. This process is repeated several times. Meditation, yoga, and listening to music are other great stress relievers. Writing about feelings in a notebook or reading an inspirational book can provide comfort and relief. Another idea is to encourage young people to ask a family member to play a game or go for a walk when they're feeling wound up. Physical activity or playing with a pet are also great ways to rid the body of tension.

POSITIVE FAMILY COMMUNICATION

Continued communication is a key factor in managing stress. **It's important for adolescents to know they have an open invitation to talk when something is bothering them.** Stress only gets worse if we pretend nothing is wrong. Young people, however, may not recognize that they're stressed. You may have to look for them to say phrases like "I'm worried," "freaked out," "tense," "wound up," "ready to burst," "coming unglued," etc.

Be there to simply listen if they have concerns and fears to tell you about. And show them affection when they express anxiety—they need your support.

When they come to you and tell you conflict with a certain person is causing them stress, encourage your children to talk with that person. If need be, help them find a self-help group, counselor, psychologist, or psychiatrist, especially if you recognize signs of depression.

A lot of stress is caused by change, even positive change. **You can try to head off stress by talking about upcoming changes.** Ask every day what's happening in your children's lives. Their information will alert you to any changes that could cause them worry.

Talk about other issues that may cause stress in a young person's life. These discussions can help prepare your children for situations they may experience, helping them to cope and relieving some stress. For example, if your son or daughter is a person of color, help your child to understand and address the issues of racism. If your child is gay or lesbian, explain the issues of homophobia and how to address discrimination.

ADULT ROLE MODELS

How do you deal with stress? Chances are your children deal with their stress based on how they've watched you, so **learn to handle pressure in your own life.** Maintain your health with what keeps stress away in the first place. Exercise regularly. Eat healthy foods. Avoid caffeine. Get enough sleep. Take a little time every day to unwind, and share some of that time with your family. Laugh at something, rent a funny movie. And don't overbook your schedule. Treat yourself to lighting a candle and playing some music that relaxes you. Through your actions, your children will see that it's important to know how to relax.

RESISTANCE SKILLS

There's much to be said for the ability to say no when it comes to stress management. When schedules are jam-packed, we often feel overwhelmed. **Help young people learn to set limits on their activities.** It's better to do a few activities well than to do a lot of things poorly while feeling stretched thin.

PLANNING AND DECISION MAKING

Adolescents obviously can't plan for everything, but planning can be a great help when it comes to stress management. **Encourage your children to think ahead about their day's schedule.** Do they have any quizzes to prepare for? Are they up to date on assignments? Have they started working on the project that's due next week? Keeping a to-do list is an excellent way to cut down on stress, and crossing out items as they are finished provides a feeling of accomplishment. Young people may want to keep track of daily goals in a journal or diary. The sense of organization and control from these simple ideas can be a real stress reducer.

GETTING RID OF THE JITTERS

Our body's natural reaction to stress is flight or fight. We can help our young people learn to cope instead. And with coping, the stomachaches from stress gradually go away—as do the jitters. We can give our children the tools to replace anxious feelings and responses with laughter and excitement. We can teach them how to bring peace into their lives.

Signs of Stress

Young people may not notice their own signs of stress. Often, physical signs of stress are mistaken as an illness. If you think your child is suffering from stress, look for some of these signals:

PHYSICAL SYMPTOMS

Nausea

Headaches

Loss of appetite or increased appetite

Rashes

Stomachaches

Fatigue

Increase in illnesses

Rapid heart rate

Dizziness

Dry mouth

Shaking

Sweating

Nail or lip biting

Frequent urination

PSYCHOLOGICAL SYMPTOMS

Lack of concentration

Forgetfulness

Decrease in school performance

Inability to study

Irritability

Carelessness

Boredom

Nightmares

Sadness or depression

Self-Acceptance

Your Dilemma:

"LaKeisha walks around with her head down most of the time. She can hardly look other people in the eye."

or

"Jamie studied all night and still got a D on his history test. He came home and said, 'I can't do anything right.'"

ACTION TIPS

◆ Help your children learn ways to boost their self-esteem. This might include carrying around notes with positive affirmations or making lists of their positive qualities.

◆ Affirm your children's positive friendships.

◆ Encourage your children to come up with a list of attainable goals and a plan for reaching them.

◆ Give your children love and support every day. Praise their achievements. When necessary, make sure it's clear that you disapprove of certain behaviors but that you love them as much as ever.

◆ Communicate how proud you are of your children. Ask questions about how things are going. Really listen to their answers.

◆ Help your community to appreciate young people as much as you do. Help create leadership roles for young people in the community. Brainstorm ideas for making the community more youth friendly.

> "The most radical act anyone can commit is to be happy."
>
> *Patch Adams*

Imagine for a moment that someone has cast a spell on you. When you wake up tomorrow morning, you will love and accept yourself completely, exactly as you are.

Not that you'll be perfect; your body, your personality, your bank account—all your life circumstances—will be just as they are today. But everything will feel different. You'll view your imperfections with tenderness and compassion. You won't feel you have to "fix" yourself in any way to be worthy of love. You'll know what it means to feel completely at ease in the world, to belong. You will simply be who you are, and that will be enough.

Now imagine that the same spell has been cast on your beloved, imperfect children. They'll feel unconditionally loved and supported and celebrate their own uniqueness and strengths. They'll unconditionally accept their flaws and limitations. Even if they don't look like supermodels or athletes, they'll know they are beautiful. They'll treat themselves with kindness and respect because they won't be ashamed of who they are. They won't feel they have to alter themselves to fit in. With this newfound confidence, they'll be able to take appropriate risks and approach life openly and with excitement. They'll be happy and at peace with themselves, exactly as they are.

The developmental assets are positive qualities, experiences, and skills that children need to grow up healthy and responsible. Parents, grandparents, stepparents, or any other guardian of a child can use these assets as a framework to help them think through the new experiences they're encountering with their children. When helping your children deal with the issue of self-acceptance and belonging, the assets you may want to consider looking at for guidance are Self-Esteem, Positive Peer Influence, Sense of Purpose, Family Support, Positive Family Communication, and Community Values Youth.

ASSET TYPE	ASSET NAME	ASSET DESCRIPTION
Positive Identity	Self-Esteem	Young people feel good about themselves.
Boundaries and Expectations	Positive Peer Influence	Young people's best friends model responsible behavior. They are a good influence. They do well at school and stay away from risky behaviors, such as alcohol and other drug use.
Positive Identity	Sense of Purpose	Young people believe that their life has a purpose.
Support	Family Support	Young people feel loved and supported in their family.
Support	Positive Family Communication	Young people turn to their parents for advice and support. They have frequent, in-depth conversations with each other on a variety of topics. Parents are approachable and available when their children want to talk.
Empowerment	Community Values Youth	Young people perceive that adults in the community value them.

SELF-ESTEEM

 It is possible to instill a sense of self-worth in young people. When we **accept them for who they are,** when we don't expect them to make up for our own failings, when we let them know we believe in them no matter what, we help them learn to love and accept themselves. We help them feel at home and at ease in the world. This doesn't mean we lower expectations for them—it means we love them just as they are and want the best for them.

You can help your children discover specific ways to boost their self-concept. The ideas that follow will help them like who they are:

- **Help them see the positive side of their personality traits.** For example, a thought such as "I'm too emotional" can be viewed as "I'm in touch with my feelings." "I'm too pushy" can become "I'm assertive and get things done."

- **Encourage them to make a list of at least 10 positive traits** and look at this list often. Many people tend to focus on their negative characteristics; it's much healthier to look at the positive.

- **Have your children make a list of past successes, whether big or small.** Suggest they look over this list periodically. Or, you may want to try making a scrapbook together of successes for each member of the family.

- **Use positive, authentic language when talking to and about your children.** Let them know what they're good at, even the little things. For example, you might comment on how responsible they are about getting to work or school on time.

- **Encourage your children to volunteer in the community or find ways to contribute to the community,** and teach them by your own example. Nothing builds self-esteem more surely than helping others.

POSITIVE PEER INFLUENCE

How young people see themselves is somewhat affected by the friends they choose. If they're surrounded by negative people—the ones who put them down—your children may find it difficult to like themselves. But if they have the kind of friends who provide support and encouragement, they are more likely to feel good about themselves. **Encourage adolescents to stick with friends who are uplifting and supportive, not negative and draining.** Help them find the positive side when you hear your children and their friends talking negatively of others in your presence.

Talk with your children about their friends. Ask ques-tions. Are they good students? Are they positive people? Do they offer you encouragement? Can you confide in them? Are they kind and honest? What types of activities do you do together? What do you like to do when you hang out?

SENSE OF PURPOSE

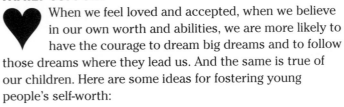 Setting goals is one way for anyone to increase her or his feelings of self-worth. **Encourage your children to think about something important they would like to accomplish, and then have them put together a plan for how to do it.** Suggest they keep track of their progress. Be careful, however, and help your children set realistic goals.

You might also suggest your children brainstorm a list of reasons to get up in the morning that includes simple pleasures, such as "to feel the warmth of the sun on my face" as well as more purposeful reasons such as "to learn something new." Suggest they find inspiring quotations about purpose, meaning, and goals and write them down in a special notebook or journal.

Spend time as a family discussing the things that give your life meaning. Ask your children what they consider to be important values. Helping others? Working hard? Making lots of money? How are these values reflected in the choices they make? Share your own views and encourage your children to revisit the questions as their views and life experiences change.

FAMILY SUPPORT

When we feel loved and accepted, when we believe in our own worth and abilities, we are more likely to have the courage to dream big dreams and to follow those dreams where they lead us. And the same is true of our children. Here are some ideas for fostering young people's self-worth:

- **Praise achievements.** Tell your children when they do a good job on something, no matter how small. Thank them for doing their share around the house.

- Be clear when you comment on behavior you don't like. **Make sure they understand you love them;** it is just the behavior with which you are unhappy.

- **Help them find what they're good at.** Can they volunteer to teach one of their skills or abilities to younger children? Is there a way they can use their skills or abilities in the neighborhood? Their involvement in the community is likely to be rewarded with recognition and appreciation.

- **Be affectionate.** Hug them if they'll let you. Ask them how they feel about physical affection, and respect their boundaries. But don't withdraw if they say they don't want affectionate displays. A touch on the arm or a pat on the back can express a lot.

- **Attend their games and performances.** Participate in school events. Show your enthusiasm and support for their interests.

- **Display their photographs, artwork, and awards** proudly and prominently in your home.

- Introduce your children to your friends, your coworkers, people in the neighborhood. **Let people know how proud you are of your children.**

POSITIVE FAMILY COMMUNICATION

Grounded in a sense of belonging and connection, we can begin to create a more spacious atmosphere of acceptance in our families. Adolescents may appear to shrug off the need for acceptance. But don't be fooled; the longing is there, as it is in each of us. Here are a few ways to let them know you recognize and love them for who they are:

- **Tell your children how proud you are of them,** and not just when they've accomplished something. Don't assume they know how you feel.

- **When your children talk, really listen.** Give them your undivided attention. If you're in the middle of something important, tell them when you'll be done, and then seek them out to follow up.

- **Eat a meal together every day if possible** or at least several times a week. Allow mealtimes to be relaxed and enjoyable, a time of sharing. Without prying, ask your children what they're thinking about, how their friends are doing, what's going on at school. Show interest in what they have to say. And talk about your day and what's on your mind.

COMMUNITY VALUES YOUTH

Our schools, neighborhoods, and communities can become places that affirm young people's sense of being valued and supported. Instead of regarding youth as problems, we can start to celebrate them as treasured resources. Here are some ideas for fostering the self-worth of youth within the community:

- **Organize a neighborhood party in honor of the young people.** Make it a special day for everyone. Ask neighbors to think of something positive and unique about each child, and present awards in recognition of each young person's strengths. Propose a toast or write a poem that expresses the idea that young people are an important part of the community. Take pictures of all the young people and make copies for them.

- **Make a video about the young people in the neighborhood,** and invite all the neighbors over to view it.

- **Get involved with your parent-teacher organization.** Talk to students about how to create a positive and supportive environment for all young people at school. Encourage teachers and administrators to get to know as many students as possible and to make a special effort to engage those who seem alienated or withdrawn.

- **Help create leadership roles for young people in the community,** such as student representatives on the school board, youth committees within the congregation, and youth advisory councils within local government. Help educate other adults about viewing young people as an asset to the community.

- **Invite people from the community to speak to students about their jobs, their travels, their hobbies.** If your school has a mentoring program, encourage friends and neighbors to participate. If not, help set up one.

- **Encourage artistic expression.** Ask a local restaurant or coffee shop to exhibit student art projects. See if a community theater has an internship program for youth. Invite a local artist to be an artist-in-residence at your child's school for a month.

- **Organize a focus group of young people to brainstorm ideas for making the community more youth friendly.** (For example, do the parks have a place for skateboarding? Could a warehouse be designated for graffiti artists?) Help young people find ways to get their ideas implemented.

- **Find ways to build cultural sensitivity within the community.** Celebrate and honor your community's differences.

ACCEPTANCE

It's so simple, really. We all want to be happy, to feel loved and accepted just as we are. With our guidance, encouragement, and unconditional love, our children can learn to celebrate who they are—and they won't even need a magic spell.

Anger Management

Your Dilemma:

**"Mei just bursts when she's upset.
She yells at me and I don't know what to do."**
or
**"Door slamming. That's what Nate does when he's mad.
He doesn't speak to us, but he slams doors."**

ACTION TIPS

◆ Let young people know that anger is normal and finding ways to resolve conflict strengthens relationships.

◆ Share ideas with them about how to avoid anger. Two suggestions include avoiding the triggers that make them angry and making an effort to change negative thoughts to positive thoughts.

◆ Talk openly about anger in your family during regular family meetings and share ideas about what to do when you recognize that you're angry.

◆ Use anger management techniques such as "I" statements, active listening, and avoiding overgeneralization.

◆ Model positive ways of handling anger and conflict appropriately.

◆ Talk to your child with respect even when you're angry with her or him.

◆ During a family meeting, come to terms on how disagreements will be handled within the family.

◆ Teach conflict-resolution skills.

◆ Set up a place of peace in your home where conflicts can be resolved.

WHAT YOUNG PEOPLE SAY: "If you don't teach by example, it won't work."

Anger is a natural emotion, but that doesn't mean it's pleasant. Whether we're the ones who are angry or someone is upset with us, anger can cause breakdowns in communication and, if not dealt with properly, hurt relationships.

When tempers flare, we may say things we don't mean. We utter phrases and words we'll regret, and in the end we look foolish. Being hot-headed has no reward. Anger can also be a mask for depression, substance abuse, and feelings of insecurity. So we need to share with our children how to keep their cool and express this normal emotion appropriately.

The developmental assets are positive qualities, experiences, and skills that children need to grow up healthy and responsible. Parents, grandparents, stepparents, or any other guardian of a child can use these assets as a framework to help them think through the new experiences they're encountering with their children. When trying to help your children deal with anger, the assets you may want to consider looking at for guidance are Personal Power, Positive Family Communication, Adult Role Models, Family Boundaries, and Peaceful Conflict Resolution.

ASSET TYPE	ASSET NAME	ASSET DESCRIPTION
Positive Identity	Personal Power	Young people feel that they have control over many things that happen to them.
Support	Positive Family Communication	Young people turn to their parents for advice and support. They have frequent, in-depth conversations with each other on a variety of topics. Parents are approachable and available when their children want to talk.
Boundaries and Expectations	Adult Role Models	Parents and other adults model positive, responsible behavior.
Boundaries and Expectations	Family Boundaries	Parents set clear rules and consequences for their children's behavior. They monitor their children's whereabouts.
Social Competencies	Peaceful Conflict Resolution	Young people seek to resolve conflicts nonviolently.

POWER

We can help our young people feel as if they have some control to avoid angry feelings in the first place. Here are suggestions you can share with them. These ideas can help you handle your own feelings as well.

- **Avoid the triggers of your anger.** If your teenage daughter doesn't like her 10-year-old sister reading her diary and they share a bedroom, tell her to hide the diary instead of leaving it out on the nightstand. If you know your child won't be able to avoid a trigger, plan ahead. Prepare her or him for the situation and the way he or she is bound to feel. Together, help your child think of as many ways to relieve the stress and pressure as you can.

- **Reframe your thoughts.** Your adolescent might be filled with negative, irrational thoughts. Teach her or him to consider whether those thoughts are fair. Your son might have the following overgeneralization running through his head, "You're never home." He could think about the truthfulness of such a feeling. He may realize his mom *is* home on Saturday and Sunday, and she does have a good talk with him every night before he goes to bed.

POSITIVE FAMILY COMMUNICATION

Talking openly about anger is one of the easiest ways to get the best of it. Regular family meetings can address issues and keep them from building up. **Share with your adolescents what to do when they recognize anger.** First, they should admit they're angry. Second, they can try to calm themselves. Some suggestions include deep breathing, writing in a journal, listening to music, and taking a walk or run. Third, they can make a choice—either take action or do nothing if the problem doesn't warrant anything being done. Finally, they should solve the problem if possible.

Once they're ready to talk, your children can use some anger management techniques like those that follow to keep the situation under control:

- Use "I" statements. Doing this avoids placing the blame on the other person. For example, instead of saying, "You're never on time," you could say, "I feel like I have to wait for you a lot."

- Practice active listening. When the other person is talking, show that you are paying attention to what is being said. Nod. Say yes when appropriate. Don't interrupt, and repeat back what he or she has just stated to show you understand.

- Watch your body language. It should match your words so that you don't send a conflicting message. For example, if you're really upset about a serious issue, don't smile as you're discussing it. The smile makes the situation seem lighter than it really is.

- Stick to the current issue. Avoid bringing up things that have happened in the past. They're irrelevant to the discussion at hand.

- Avoid overgeneralizing. Pay attention to your words. Are you using phrases such as "you always" and "you never?" These are inaccurate, unfair, and unhelpful.

- Avoid "yes, but . . ." and substitute "yes, and . . . ."

ADULT ROLE MODELS

How we handle our own anger is reflected in how our children handle theirs. **As models, we need to show them that anger is okay if expressed appropriately.** When we show anger, we must use self-restraint and express our feelings in proportion to the problem. If you are concerned about your own (or your partner's) anger or violence within your family, seek counsel from a trusted professional, such as a counselor, religious leader, or doctor.

When you are upset with your children, talk to them with respect. This action demonstrates how we should treat others when we're angry. Use a variety of words, such as *irritated, annoyed,* or *frustrated,* to model for your children the range of feelings that anger can take.

If you're in the middle of a disagreement, and your child yells or speaks disrespectfully, you might simply walk away after giving a calm and quiet response. It's important to communicate that such behavior is not acceptable and is not a way to solve problems. Resume the conversation when everyone is calmer.

FAMILY BOUNDARIES

Have a family meeting and agree on how you will expect one another to act when disagreements occur. The following are good ground rules:

- Avoid bringing up past problems once they're resolved. If your daughter came home late one night in February and you dealt with it then, avoid bringing up the situation five or six months later.

- Be clear that when you're upset, you dislike the *behavior*, not the person.

- Agree to wait to talk until both parties are feeling calmer. Give everyone a chance to cool down.

- Try to be objective. Try to see the situation from the other person's point of view. Are you acting rationally?

PEACEFUL CONFLICT RESOLUTION

Anger often goes hand in hand with conflict, and the process of working through conflict often strengthens relationships and builds understanding. Therefore, **it's important that we teach young people ways to resolve conflict peacefully.** When a conflict occurs in your family, everyone involved should state their needs and wants without blaming others. The next step is for everyone to really listen and focus on understanding each other. It's important that during the discussion, everyone stays focused on the conflict at hand and doesn't bring up other conflicts. Use creative problem solving to find new solutions. Try spending some time brainstorming solutions together, and consider each one. Work together until you reach a situation in which everybody wins.

You can set up a "peace room" in your home. This location could be a room or section of a room where family members can go when they need to resolve a conflict or cool down. You probably will want to set ground rules for your place of peace. These might include going there together if someone asks you to, using only respectful words, taking turns talking and listening, using I-statements, and getting help if the problem is too big for you to solve.

FINDING THE CALM

Adolescents are experiencing a time of great hormonal and physical changes, and anger naturally comes as part of the package. Anger isn't a bad emotion; it's a normal one. But without support and guidance, adolescents may not know how to handle anger's powerful and raw feelings. With parental love and support, however, they can learn how to live with anger and deal with conflict in a way that keeps their world a little calmer.

Talking about Anger

Positive communication about anger can help avoid conflicts. Here are some questions you and your family may want to discuss to find out how each member feels about anger and its causes before the next conflict arises:

- What do you think about when you hear the word *anger*?
- What makes you angry?
- What goes on in your mind when you're angry?
- Describe a time when someone was angry with you. What did he or she do? How did you feel? What was the outcome?
- Do you think stress is sometimes a factor when people get angry?
- What causes stress in your life?
- How could you better manage this stress? How could family members help?
- How could you keep the things that make you angry from being destructive?
- What could you do to calm down when you're angry?
- What helps you relax?
- How does our culture express anger?
- How *do* we, as a family, handle anger?
- How *could* we, as a family, handle anger more constructively?

Depression

Your Dilemma:

"First Allison's tearful; then she's short-tempered. It's been going back and forth like this for almost a month. In the morning, it's nearly impossible to get her out of bed. She hasn't washed her hair, called her friends, or eaten much of anything for a couple of days. She doesn't even want to go shopping. Is this just a 'phase'?"

ACTION TIPS

◆ Remember that depression is treatable. If you're concerned that your child (or another young person in your life) is depressed, seek professional help right away.

◆ Remember that depression is a medical condition, not a character flaw. Be supportive and patient with a loved one who is depressed.

◆ Take care of your own needs, too. It isn't easy to take care of someone who is depressed. Join a support group, talk to friends or a counselor about it, or keep a journal. Find ways to lighten your own load.

◆ Foster your adolescent's self-esteem. Be generous with hugs and encouragement, and help your child recognize that depression is an illness that does not diminish her or his worth in any way.

◆ Be optimistic about the future. Without denying the present difficulty, help create an atmosphere of hope and acceptance for your child.

◆ Learn to recognize the symptoms of depression, and be alert to them in the young people you know. Educate them about the signs, too. They may be the first to tell you that they feel depressed.

◆ Educate others who work with young people. Share what you've learned with teachers, school counselors, and other parents.

◆ You can find many good books about living with depression at the library or bookstore, too.

WHAT YOUNG PEOPLE SAY: *"Reassure me and encourage me."*

Depression is a serious medical condition that causes an overwhelming sense of sadness and despair. The pain of depression can keep a person from functioning. Yet depression can be very difficult to identify, particularly in young people. Telling the difference between an adolescent who is merely sad and one who is severely depressed can take a careful eye—and may require the help of a trained mental health professional.

Being alert to the symptoms of depression in the young is extremely important. Getting proper treatment can literally be a matter of life and death: Untreated depression puts adolescents at risk for suicide.

Fortunately, a great deal of help is available. Depression is a highly treatable condition that responds to a variety of treatments, including medications and other types of therapy. Young people who are depressed need professional help and support from everyone who cares about them.

The developmental assets are positive qualities, experiences, and skills that children need to grow up healthy and responsible. Parents, grandparents, stepparents, or any other guardian of a child can use these assets as a framework to help them think through the new experiences they're encountering with their children. When dealing with depression in your family, the assets you may want to consider looking at for guidance are Positive Family Communication, Family Support, Other Adult Relationships, Caring School Climate, Personal Power, Self-Esteem, and Positive View of Personal Future.

ASSET TYPE	ASSET NAME	ASSET DESCRIPTION
Support	Positive Family Communication	Young people turn to their parents for advice and support. They have frequent, in-depth conversations with each other on a variety of topics. Parents are approachable and available when their children want to talk.
Support	Family Support	Young people feel loved and supported in their family.
Support	Other Adult Relationships	Young people know other adults besides their parents they can turn to for advice and support. They have frequent, in-depth conversations with them. Ideally, three or more adults play this role in their lives.
Support	Caring School Climate	Young people feel that their school supports them, encourages them, and cares about them.
Positive Identity	Personal Power	Young people feel that they have control over many things that happen to them.
Positive Identity	Self-Esteem	Young people feel good about themselves.
Positive Identity	Positive View of Personal Future	Young people are optimistic about their own future.

POSITIVE FAMILY COMMUNICATION

Good communication is crucial in identifying and helping young people who are depressed. **The more aware you are of your son or daughter's typical mood and outlook, the better you'll be able to judge whether there has been a change for the worse.** Checking in with each other every day keeps you aware of your child's present mood and also provides her or him with a sense of security and comfort. They may not always act like it, but adolescents really need to know that adults are paying attention to what's going on with them. Make sure your child knows the signs of depression. (See the list on page 5.) Young people can spot it in themselves, too.

If you're concerned that your child may be depressed, **pay close attention to nonverbal cues, such as changes in appearance, attitude, and behavior.** Ask your child questions about what you're observing. Voice your concerns to others who have regular contact with her or him. Find out whether your child's friends, teachers, or coaches have noticed mood changes and other symptoms of depression.

If a number of symptoms have been present for more than two weeks, don't wait to see if your child "snaps out of it." **Get help right away.** If you don't know of a good therapist or psychiatrist, see if your regular doctor can make a referral for you. You might also see if your company has an employee assistance program that can help, or try a crisis intervention service available by phone.

FAMILY SUPPORT

A young person who is depressed needs a great deal of support. You can help by remembering that depression is an illness and not a character flaw. Give your son or daughter extra love and affection. Small gestures of kindness can mean a lot when someone is suffering. You might pick some flowers and put them in your child's room for example. Or, leave a little note about some trait you admire in your child. **Make a point of spending time together, without expecting her or him to be cheerful.**

Learn about depression. Ask your doctor for patient-information materials about the illness, or do some research at the library or on the Internet. Share what you learn with family members and other people who care about your child.

If your child is prescribed medication to treat depression, **be sure you understand the dosage requirements** and any other information that may affect the drug's effectiveness. Because depression can make it seem as though nothing matters, following a medication regimen may be hard for your child. So help keep track of the schedule and make sure he or she is taking every dose. Sometimes medication takes a few days to several weeks to take full effect.

Ask your friends to help support you through this crisis, to let you express your fears and frustrations with them so that you don't feel compelled to do so with your child. When he or she is depressed, it's easy to feel like the worst parent in the world. But don't focus on blaming yourself. Depression is a disease that is no one's fault and that cannot be prevented. Be sure to pay attention to your own needs, and learn to recognize when you need a break. Try to get some exercise every day and get plenty of rest. These measures will help give you the emotional and physical stamina you need to help your child.

OTHER ADULT RELATIONSHIPS

Reach out to other people who have experienced depression themselves or have helped a loved one get through it. Ask them for ideas about coping. Ask a trusted relative, friend, or neighbor to spend time with your son or daughter on a regular basis, doing something easy and fun together—such as going to a movie. Encourage your child to talk about how things are going.

CARING SCHOOL CLIMATE

Make sure your child's school staff and faculty are aware of her or his depression. Then teachers, guidance counselors, and the school nurse can be alert to distress signals and can provide additional support and guidance. If you find that the school seems uninformed about depression and its consequences, make an effort to educate them. Talk to the administration about conducting an in-service training for staff on depression in adolescents. Everyone who works with young people should be properly informed about the topic.

PERSONAL POWER

Depression can temporarily rob young people of a sense of their own power. They may feel they have no control over what happens to them and that there's no hope of life getting better. **Reassure your child that depression is a treatable condition** and that, together, you'll get through this difficult time. Help her or him find ways to feel better in the short term. For example, regular exercise can help counteract depression, so invite your child to go for regular walks with you.

SELF-ESTEEM

Regardless of the type of treatment your child receives, it's wise to be mindful of helping to **strengthen her or his self-esteem.** Self-acceptance can be difficult under any circumstances, but depression takes a toll on a person's self-image, and rebuilding it may take some extra effort.

Ask your son or daughter to help you make a scrapbook about things you each like about yourself. Cut out pictures from magazines and talk about what they mean to each of you. Make a book together that reflects positive feelings of self-care.

Invite your child to help you in some type of service to others. Volunteering time to helping others can be a great boost to a young person's self-esteem.

POSITIVE VIEW OF PERSONAL FUTURE

Help young people remember that these present difficulties are temporary. Things are painful right now, but the future is full of hope. **Inspire optimism in your child by being optimistic yourself.** Avoid making gloomy predictions or dwelling on negative circumstances or outcomes. As much as possible, focus on hopeful events in the community and the world, and bring these to your

family's attention. Post articles on the refrigerator that profile people who are contributing to the world in a positive way. Plant a garden together. Spend time outdoors, enjoying the beauty of nature. Visit places, such as peace gardens or places of worship, that inspire a sense of hope.

THE SHINING WORLD

Coping with a serious illness such as depression is a tremendous challenge for patients as well as the people who love them. Young people who are struggling with depression need ongoing support—from a trained mental health professional, from their family and friends, and from their school.

Depression is a frightening and painful experience, yet there is triumph in overcoming it. In his memoir of depression, *Darkness Visible*, William Styron* likens the condition to the poet Dante's descent into Hell, and the return to health as a return to what Dante calls "the shining world." Styron points out that countless people have made this courageous and difficult journey, and he concludes his tale with these words of hope from the poet:

And so we came forth, and once again
beheld the stars.

* Styron, William. *Darkness Visible: A Memoir of Madness.* New York: Vintage Books, 1990.

DID YOU KNOW?

Girls are twice as vulnerable to depression as boys are.

From: Healthy Teen Development Seminar by Laurence Steinberg, Ph.D

Symptoms of Depression

It's a good idea for parents and young people to be familiar with the symptoms of depression.** Some of the symptoms you can see; others you have to ask about. If you suspect your adolescent is depressed, don't hesitate to ask about her or his frame of mind. (If you think one of your child's friends may be depressed, share your concerns with the young person's parents.) Seek professional help right away if four or more of the following statements are true for at least a two-week period:

- The young person appears depressed most of the time (i.e., most of the time during most days).

- He or she either reports feeling sad or hopeless or frequently appears tearful or upset.

- He or she shows little or no interest in daily activities most of the time.

- He or she has gained or lost a significant amount of weight (a change of more than five percent in body weight) in a month; he or she overeats or eats too little nearly every day.

- He or she is easily distracted or has an inability to concentrate.

- He or she has trouble sleeping or trouble staying awake nearly every day.

- He or she either moves slowly or appears agitated most of the time. (Young people who are depressed may be extremely touchy or irritable.)

- He or she has changes in grades.

- He or she appears excessively tired most of the time.

- He or she has feelings of worthlessness or excessive guilt nearly every day.

- He or she has trouble concentrating or making decisions most of the time.

- He or she has recurrent thoughts about death and suicide or has a plan to commit suicide.

** Symptoms are summarized from: American Psychiatric Association. (1994). *Diagnostic and statistical manual of mental disorders,* fourth edition. Washington, D.C., American Psychiatric Association.

40 Ways to Show Young People You Care

1. Notice them.

2. Smile at them.

3. Look them in the eye when you talk to them.

4. Ask them about themselves.

5. Let them tell you how they feel.

6. Tell them what you like about them.

7. Ask their opinions.

8. Seek them out.

9. Give them your undivided attention.

10. Hug them.

11. Notice when they're acting differently.

12. Tolerate their interruptions.

13. Accept them as they are.

14. Tell them how much you like being with them.

15. Make yourself available.

16. Be nice to them.

17. Be honest with them.

18. Keep the promises you make to them.

19. Tell them what you expect of them.

20. Respect them.

21. Believe in them.

22. Make time to be with them.

23. Be excited when you see them.

24. Notice when they grow.

25. Remember their birthdays.

26. Introduce them to your friends.

27. Include them in conversations.

28. Do what they like to do.

29. Listen to their favorite music with them.

30. Read aloud together.

31. Go places together.

32. Build something together.

33. Make decisions together.

34. Help them learn something new.

35. Ask them to help you with something.

36. Encourage them to help others.

37. Let them make mistakes.

38. Admit when you make a mistake.

39. Tell them how proud you are of them.

40. Encourage them to think big.

Jobs Outside the Home

Your Dilemma:

"Melanie's grades have dropped since last semester; last term, she wasn't working 20 hours a week."

or

"Tran wants a stereo, but we think he should earn it. Should we ask him to get a job?"

ACTION TIPS

◆ Be sure your adolescent's job schedule allows enough time at home and enough time for schoolwork and other obligations. It's a good idea to limit an adolescent's work schedule to 15 hours per week.

◆ Allow your children to learn their own lessons about responsibility. Avoid trying to rescue them from their own mistakes (e.g., by giving them rides to work more than once when their own poor planning makes them late).

◆ Help them learn money-management skills. Show them how to create a budget, and help them set up a savings account. Talk to them about the importance of saving for the future.

◆ Ask questions about how work is going, how they're getting along with their coworkers, and whether they feel good about the work they do. Having someone to talk to about the day-to-day events of the workplace helps young people put these encounters in the proper context and make the most of what they learn from their work experience.

WHAT YOUNG PEOPLE SAY: "Help me balance my time in the things I'm interested in (dancing, writing, hanging out with friends) and the things I have to do (school, job, chores)."

Working a part-time job can teach a young person many valuable lessons. Responsibility, time management, and getting along with other people are just a few of the important skills and values working can impart. But the benefits have to be weighed carefully against the drawbacks. Each young person's situation and abilities are unique. Some adolescents can handle a full academic schedule, involvement in extracurricular activities, and a job. Others can't—at least not yet.

The developmental assets are positive qualities, experiences, and skills that children need to grow up healthy and responsible. Parents, grandparents, stepparents, or any other guardian of a child can use these assets as a framework to help them think through the new experiences they're encountering with their children. When dealing with the issue of jobs outside the home in your family, the assets and larger asset categories you may want to consider looking at for guidance are Constructive Use of Time, Positive Family Communication, Responsibility, Planning and Decision Making, Sense of Purpose, and Interpersonal Competence.

ASSET TYPE	ASSET NAME	ASSET DESCRIPTION
Constructive Use of Time	Asset #17 Creative Activities Asset #18 Youth Programs Asset #19 Religious Community Asset #20 Time at Home	Young people need constructive, enriching opportunities for growth through creative activities, youth programs, congregational involvement, and quality time at home.
Support	Positive Family Communication	Young people turn to their parents for advice and support. They have frequent, in-depth conversations with each other on a variety of topics. Parents are approachable and available when their children want to talk.
Positive Values	Responsibility	Young people accept and take personal responsibility for their actions and decisions.
Social Competencies	Planning and Decision Making	Young people know how to plan ahead and make choices.
Positive Identity	Sense of Purpose	Young people believe that their life has a purpose.
Social Competencies	Interpersonal Competence	Young people have empathy, sensitivity, and friendship skills.

CONSTRUCTIVE USE OF TIME

Some families don't have a choice; they need the additional income of a working child. Other families find themselves in a different situation and a job basically means extra spending money for a child. In either case, **consider how a job affects the balance of home life, schoolwork, and other activities in a young person's life.** Does your child have enough time for schoolwork and other responsibilities, as well as time for social, spiritual, and physical development? A young person who is already struggling in school probably shouldn't take on the additional responsibility of a job. And if your child seems to be falling behind as a result of working, you may need to reevaluate the situation.

Limit a job to no more than 15 hours per week. Young people who work more than this tend to do poorly in school and are deprived of much-needed sleep. They also do not have enough time at home with family. Even if your adolescent is working, it's still important to spend time together as a family. Have a family meal together at least several nights a week.

POSITIVE FAMILY COMMUNICATION

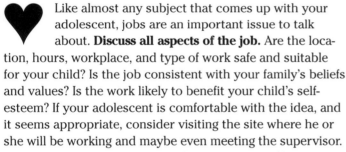

Like almost any subject that comes up with your adolescent, jobs are an important issue to talk about. **Discuss all aspects of the job.** Are the location, hours, workplace, and type of work safe and suitable for your child? Is the job consistent with your family's beliefs and values? Is the work likely to benefit your child's self-esteem? If your adolescent is comfortable with the idea, and it seems appropriate, consider visiting the site where he or she will be working and maybe even meeting the supervisor.

Talk with your child about the importance of keeping up with grades and schoolwork, staying involved in extracurricular activities, and maintaining a social life. **Life shouldn't become all about the job.**

Ask how work is going—on a regular basis. Discussions might pop up about how to handle conflict with coworkers and how and why certain procedures are done. Such discussions are learning experiences for your child and can help make a tedious job more interesting.

RESPONSIBILITY

Having a part-time job can be a great way for young people to feel a stronger sense of responsibility and freedom. Being accountable for their work habits and sticking to a schedule will help them gain valuable experience of the world beyond family and school.

For young people to benefit fully from the experience of having a job, they need to assume total responsibility for all that it entails. For example, getting to work on time is a key

responsibility. If this is consistently a problem for your child, he or she is likely to hear about it from the boss. **Resist the urge to come to the rescue more than once** and provide last-minute rides to work to keep your adolescent from being late. Facing the consequences of her or his actions is an important part of learning responsible behavior.

Your child may start a job and want to quit. Discuss why he or she feels this way. If it's simply a matter of "I don't feel like doing this work," try to find ways to inspire her or him to stick with the job.

PLANNING AND DECISION MAKING

Working outside the home can also teach young people some crucial lessons about time management. Juggling the competing responsibilities of family, school, other activities, and work can be challenging at any age, and young people may find it a struggle. **Help your children learn how to plan their time.** For example, provide a day planner and show them how to use it. You might also spend some time at the beginning of each week discussing everyone's schedule for the coming week. (Sunday night can be a good time to do this.) Post a family calendar in a prominent place and have everyone mark each day's activities on it.

A job can also provide young people with an opportunity to learn about financial management. **Talk to your children about how to make the best use of their paychecks.** Show them how to create a budget, and help them set up a savings account. If they decide to get a checking account, be sure they know how to balance their checkbook. Emphasize the importance of setting aside money for savings and giving to charitable causes. Consider having them help contribute toward gas and auto insurance if they use the car. For some young people a job simply provides spending money. These young people may feel the temptation of having extra cash, and work may become more important than school. Therefore, it's important to explain to your children about expenses they can expect as adults. That way, a short-term job and the money it provides may be less likely to compete with their education.

SENSE OF PURPOSE

Having a sense of purpose in life is important at any age, and a job can contribute to this feeling. **Talk to your children about whether their job feels meaningful and worthwhile or is "just a job."** Ask what kind of job would provide the greatest sense of accomplishment? Would he or she rather be working in a law office than at a fast-food restaurant? Is service to others part of the picture, or is making money the main objective? There is no one right answer, but it's important to ask the questions.

Although many jobs available to young people may seem of a menial nature, even these tasks can be meaningful if they are approached with a sense of purpose. Opportunities to help others, to provide good service, and to be part of a team can make even the most repetitive job worthwhile.

INTERPERSONAL COMPETENCE

A job can also teach young people a great deal about working with others. Getting along with a wide variety of people and taking an interest in other people's lives and stories are important skills in any situation, and the workplace provides many opportunities for honing these abilities. **Learning to follow instructions, accepting criticism, and dealing with difficult people are just a few of the tough lessons a job can teach.**

You can help your child profit from these experiences by providing a safe place to "process" the events of the workday. **Talking through an encounter with an employer or coworker can be a great help to a young person** who is trying to sort out all of the confusing interactions that can occur when people work together.

POWER OVER THE FUTURE

Having and keeping a job can provide a sense of optimism about the future. Knowing that they're capable of working hard and succeeding at what they set out to do can give young people a sense of security about their own abilities. And earning a regular paycheck can nurture the sense that they'll be able to provide for themselves when they make the move to living independently.

Encourage your children to view the future optimistically. Emphasize the importance of their own actions in creating the kind of life they want to live. The more they recognize the importance of their own choices and the power they have over those choices, the more they're likely to feel that they can do whatever they set out to do.

Money

Your Dilemma:

"Even though she gets an allowance, Becca ends up asking for more cash by the end of the week."

or

"Justin has a job and earns his own money, but he spends it all on magazines and junk food."

ACTION TIPS

◆ Be aware of your own attitudes toward money. If money is consistently a problem in your life, take steps to create a more positive relationship with your finances. Take a money-management class, join a support group, get some credit counseling, or talk to a financial manager.

◆ Talk to young people about money. Don't make it a taboo topic. Discuss financial realities in both general and specific terms—from the prices of specific items to the distribution of wealth in our society. For example, what do they think about teachers' salaries in comparison to those of professional athletes? Ask their input on important purchases, such as cars and vacations.

◆ Work on a family budget, using actual or hypothetical numbers. Work with your children to create a realistic budget so they begin to get an idea of what it takes to run a household. The next time you have to draft a budget for something—a trip, for example, ask your children to work with you on it.

◆ Share the shopping duties. Let older children be responsible for grocery shopping and meal preparation one week a month. (Younger children can pitch in, too.) This is a great way to learn about financial management, responsibility, and planning ahead.

◆ Encourage good money habits. Help your children start to think of their paychecks or allowance as actual income, to be handled wisely. Encourage them to open a savings account, show them how to create a personal budget (with money set aside for fun and for savings), and talk to them about the importance of donating money to charitable organizations or causes they care about.

FACT: Young people who have more developmental assets
report making more sound choices related to money.

From: Search Institute

Money: It makes the world go 'round. Love of it is the root of all evil. It doesn't grow on trees. It's power; it's freedom. It's dirty; it's precious. We hate it; we love it. We wish we had more; we wish it didn't matter.

But it does.

Like it or not, money matters a great deal. Our attitudes about it affect the way we live, the choices we make, and sometimes even our feelings about our own worth. And we pass on these attitudes to our children, usually without even being aware we're doing so.

Yet despite its importance, what we generally *don't* pass along to our children is training in how to *handle* money. Most young people, like most parents, never receive any real education about even the most basic money-management skills, such as creating a budget or balancing a check-book. Relatively few high schools offer classes in personal finance, and those that do usually don't require them. Somehow, we're all just supposed to know how to handle money.

The developmental assets are positive qualities, experiences, and skills that children need to grow up healthy and responsible. Parents, grandparents, stepparents, or any other guardian of a child can use these assets as a framework to help them think through the new experiences they're encountering with their children. When dealing with the issue of money in your family, the assets and larger asset categories you may want to consider looking at for guidance are Adult Role Models, Commitment to Learning, Positive Family Communication, Support, and Planning and Decision Making. or balancing a checkbook

ASSET TYPE	ASSET NAME	ASSET DESCRIPTION
Boundaries and Expectations	Adult Role Models	Parents and other adults model positive, responsible behavior.
Commitment to Learning	Asset #21 Achievement Motivation Asset #22 School Engagement Asset #23 Homework Asset #24 Bonding to School Asset #25 Reading for Pleasure	Young people need to develop a lifelong commitment to education and learning.
Support	Positive Family Communication	Young people turn to their parents for advice and support. They have frequent, in-depth conversations with each other on a variety of topics. Parents are approachable and available when their children want to talk.
Support	Asset #1 Family Support Asset #2 Positive Family Communication Asset #3 Other Adult Relationships Asset #4 Caring Neighborhood Asset #5 Caring School Climate Asset #6 Parent Involvement in Schooling	Young people need to experience support, care, and love from their families and many others. They need organizations and institutions that provide positive, supportive environments.
Social Competencies	Planning and Decision Making	Young people know how to plan ahead and make choices.

ADULT ROLE MODELS

If you're completely at ease with all matters financial, consider yourself truly fortunate. For you, sharing your skills and knowledge with young people is a matter of making the time. For the rest of us, however, the situation tends to be stickier, and it's a topic we often would like to avoid. Regardless, we need to help young people learn how to handle money and make it a positive aspect of their lives.

- **Be a role model for giving.** By example, you can help encourage your children to give a certain amount of their money to worthy causes throughout the year.

- **Model responsible spending when out on shopping trips with your children,** and talk about how you come to your shopping decisions.

COMMITMENT TO LEARNING

Taking a money-management class can be an extremely worthwhile investment. You can also find many good books and tapes on the subject. And financial consultants, counselors, and support groups can be a big help for people struggling with money issues. Be compassionate with yourself in this process; taking responsibility for your financial circumstances is likely to be challenging. Often, tackling the emotional component of dealing with money is harder than learning the practical skills.

Regardless of how you go about improving your financial self-assurance, you can be sure that you won't be the only one who will benefit from your efforts. Your courage and willingness to explore this difficult terrain will set a powerful example for your children. Your leadership in this area is priceless.

POSITIVE FAMILY COMMUNICATION

Like most taboo topics, money becomes less mysterious when it's dealt with more openly. Here are some ideas for helping your children become more familiar and comfortable with financial matters.

Include money in your regular family discussions. Let these conversations range from the specific—the price of movie tickets, for example—to the general—say, the importance of being an informed consumer and recognizing whether advertising makes us want items we don't need. Discuss the messages young people receive about money in different settings, such as at school, with friends, in the media, etc. For example, talk about how the messages sent by the media affect their consumer choices. Help explain your cultural community's view of money and how it's to be used or allocated. Be honest about your own attitudes regarding money, and talk about the ones you're trying to change. If you're in debt or on financial assistance, explain how this works and what your plans are for moving ahead. If money is tight, explain how you stretch it. Teach your children how to be careful with spending and how to work toward a more financially sound future.

Ask for your children's input on important purchases, such as cars and vacations. Keep these family conversations open and relaxed.

Talk to your children about the importance of contributing to a charity or cause of their choosing. Such donations not only benefit the recipient, but also increase the donor's self-esteem and build a sense of the good that can come from responsible money management.

Discuss what can happen if life circumstances change. Talk about how you prepare for uncontrollable situations such as medical emergencies or job loss.

SUPPORT

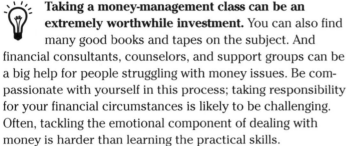

The family needn't be a young person's only source of information about financial management. Ideally, helping young people learn how to handle money can become a part of their broader education. Here are some ideas for bringing in more resources.

Talk to friends and neighbors. Are there people you know who have some financial expertise they'd be willing to share with young people? Maybe you have a friend who can discuss the importance of long-term savings, explain the ins and outs of investments, or simply demonstrate how to balance a checkbook. You might see if your friend would be willing to talk to a group of young people informally in your home. Or, if handling money is something you're good at, share what you know with others through a school or community program.

Talk to your child's school. Schools need to be aware that money management is an essential life skill for young adults. Work with your school's parent organization or with individual teachers or guidance counselors to encourage the development of an age-appropriate personal-finance course.

Talk to your local bank. See if your community bank would be interested in offering a free money-management seminar to adolescents from your school or neighborhood. An afternoon workshop could address the issues of creating a budget, managing a checkbook, and building a savings account. Perhaps some local businesses would be willing to match the young people's savings (up to $25 each, for example) to enable them to open a savings account. The youth gain a better understanding of money management, the bank gains new customers, and the community gains better-informed citizens who aren't intimidated by the prospect of dealing with money.

PLANNING AND DECISION MAKING

 The earlier young people learn to deal with money in a healthy and positive way, the better off they'll be in the long run.

Work out a family budget. Your children don't need to know every detail of your finances, but it's important for them to become aware of basic expenses—rent or mortgage, insurance, utilities, groceries, clothing, etc. (If you prefer, you can do this as a hypothetical budget.) Seeing how far a paycheck has to stretch will probably surprise them. They'll be much less shocked by what it takes to get by when they get out on their own—and possibly more appreciative of what they have while they're still at home. If your children have jobs, you may want them to contribute a reasonable amount of their paycheck toward the family's expenses.

Help your children create a personal budget. Encourage them to begin thinking of their own money (whether it's from an allowance or a part-time job) as real income to be handled with respect and care. Help them consider their expenses, set aside money for fun, and think about their long-term goals (such as saving up for a stereo, car, or college).

Share the shopping duties. Let your older children be responsible for the grocery shopping and dinner preparation one week a month. Give them a reasonable budget to work within, and have them plan the dinner menus, do the shopping (even if you have to drive them there), and prepare the meals. They'll need help at first, of course, but they'll probably enjoy the feeling of autonomy that comes with responsibility. And they'll quickly learn what a challenge it is to feed a family on a limited budget.

Encourage good money habits. Emphasize the importance of starting a savings account, and encourage them to think about how much they can put away each week or month. If they want to save for something specific, that's great. But encourage them to start putting money into a more general savings account as well.

Help your children understand the concept of sharing resources. In some cultural communities, it is common to share resources, such as money. For example, some families might pool their money together to obtain certain family needs, such as a car.

Teach them about credit card use. Share tips with your children, such as recording each purchase as if it were a checking account entry and paying off their bill monthly, instead of letting a balance add up. Teach them about the impact of high interest rates and late payment fees. Be sure your children understand the dangers of running up large amounts of credit card debt.

SOUND INVESTMENT

The bottom line, so to speak, is that young people need our help learning to be on friendly terms with money. Regardless of the path they choose in life—whether they become artists or bankers, teachers or carpenters—we want their relationship with money to be harmonious and empowering. We want them to know they have choices about money, that they are capable of handling it, that there is such a thing as having enough. We want them to earn enough to be comfortable, spend wisely, enjoy what they have, and save for the future. We want their lives to be happy and prosperous.

Questions to Help Your Family Discuss Money Matters

Many (if not most) people muddle along in a complex and emotionally charged relationship with money. The truth for many otherwise confident and competent adults is that money frightens us. So much so, in fact, that many people are more comfortable talking about sex than about financial matters. Whether this is true for you or not, there's a good chance that money isn't a topic you discuss freely with your children. For the most part, we don't discuss our income, we keep our worries to ourselves, and we don't share what we do know about how money works. Here are some questions that can help you and your children toward a frank discussion about financial matters:

1. How do you feel about money?

2. How important is money?

3. What money or other resources do you need to achieve your personal, family, or cultural community goals?

4. Are you taking the steps necessary now to earn and save money so that you can achieve your goals later? What kinds of activities are you doing?

5. Do you think having a budget is a good idea? Why or why not?

6. What do you currently know about banking? What would you like to learn?

7. Do you try to save some of your money? Why or why not?

8. What are your savings goals? (If you don't have any just yet, what might some of these future goals be?)

9. Is it important to do things with your money that help other people (such as give to charity or support causes such as human rights)? Why or why not?

10. How have you seen adults model giving money to charity? What have you learned?

11. Do you think of yourself as a smart consumer most of the time? Why or why not?

12. How often do you buy something impulsively?

13. Do you think credit cards are a good idea? Why or why not?

14. Do you think going into debt is a problem in our society? Why or why not?

15. When you think about earning money now or in the future, do you focus more on how much you want to earn or how you want to earn it? Why is this so?

Appearance

Your Dilemma:

"Honey! Your hair! It's pink!"
"Magenta. And it's only the tips."
"Right. Magenta. Interesting effect."
"I knew you'd be like this."

ACTION TIPS

◆ Learn to be flexible when setting boundaries and take the long view. Pink hair today may be brown again tomorrow.

◆ Have a relaxed discussion about appearance and fashion trends. Share some of your funny stories of being a fashion victim.

◆ Share with your adolescent what trends pose a potential health risk, such as piercing. Discuss both the pros and cons.

◆ Emphasize positive character traits rather than appearance.

◆ Actively listen to what messages your children are trying to send about themselves through what they wear.

◆ Ask and listen to how your children see their dress as reflecting on the family or community.

WHAT YOUNG PEOPLE SAY: "Give me the chance to be 'cool,' to be recognized as a beautiful individual, no matter how I look."

Body piercing, tattoos, dramatic hairstyles, and unconventional clothing are all part of youth culture. For many young people, exotic attire is an important part of their emerging personal identity. So where is the line drawn between healthy self-expression and bizarrely antisocial behavior? How do you set reasonable limits yet leave room for each child's unique personality?

Of course, there is no one right answer. What works for one family may not work for another. But by being honest about our own reactions and defining clear boundaries, it's possible to come up with some useful guidelines for what's okay—while respecting and supporting our adolescents' individuality.

The developmental assets are positive qualities, experiences, and skills that children need to grow up healthy and responsible. Parents, grandparents, stepparents, or any other guardian of a child can use these assets as a framework to help them think through the new experiences they're encountering with their children. When dealing with the issue of appearance in your family, the assets you may want to consider looking at for guidance are Family Boundaries, Positive Family Communication, Safety, and Self-Esteem.

ASSET TYPE	ASSET NAME	ASSET DESCRIPTION
Boundaries and Expectations	Family Boundaries	Parents set clear rules and consequences for their children's behavior. They monitor their children's whereabouts.
Support	Positive Family Communication	Young people can and do turn to their parents for advice and support. They have frequent, in-depth conversations with each other on a variety of topics. Parents are approachable and available when their children want to talk.
Empowerment	Safety	Young people feel safe at home, at school, and in their neighborhood.
Positive Identity	Self-Esteem	Young people feel good about themselves.

FAMILY BOUNDARIES

As parents, we often feel that our children are a reflection of ourselves: If *they* look bad, *we* look bad. A child's misbehavior can seem like a direct affront to our parenting skills. And an adolescent's fashion statement can seem like an insult. (Surely those enormous orange pants with the big zippers all over them were designed for the express purpose of embarrassing the wearer's parents. Ditto the furry green hat.)

It's important to recognize that part of what they're doing is defining their separation from you, which is a natural and healthy part of growing up. They also may simply be trying to fit in with their peers. Of course, they may also be trying to embarrass you, and in this case, a sense of humor comes in handy. The more secure you are in yourself, the more relaxed you'll be about your child's appearance, and the less likely that your daughter's shaved head will rock your world.

Spend some time thinking about your own attitudes regarding your child's appearance. You may be surprised by what you discover. Learn to recognize and respect your own boundaries, then discuss them with your child. Give her or him the chance to tell you what he or she thinks of their fairness. **Be willing to learn and change.** Reflect on your own thoughts of why you don't like your child's new look. Is it simply because it doesn't fit your style and your "image"? Or, does the concern go deeper and deal with issues such as values and safety? Be flexible where you can—but if you just can't handle the thought of Stacy wearing her nose-ring to Great Aunt Edna's birthday party, it's okay to draw the line.

POSITIVE FAMILY COMMUNICATION

Good communication skills are essential in creating a workable "dress code" for your family. An agreement reached through open and caring discussion is much more likely to be upheld than a strict order.

Approach the topic with an open mind and an attitude of mutual respect. Keep in mind that what may look appalling and outlandish to you may be the height of fashion among your child's friends. You might want to share stories about some of your own fashion experiments from the teenage years. Be creative when discussing the advantages and disadvantages of appearance alterations that are more or less permanent, such as tattoos. You could ask your children to consider how their tastes change. Would they wear today a style they liked six months ago? Ask them to imagine a really great tattoo on their grandmother's upper arm and see what their reaction is.

Try to listen without judgment to what your child tells you. Remember that fashion really is a matter of taste, and we don't all have to agree on what looks good.

We do all have to reach some agreement on what's acceptable, however. **A relaxed and open discussion will give you the opportunity to explore a number of important concerns with your child.** For example, consider whether the mode of dress or adornment in question is:

- safe, or does it involve a possible health risk?
- more or less permanent in its effect?
- sexually inappropriate or otherwise offensive (such as T-shirt slogans that make use of profanity)?
- a sign of allegiance to a particular group or gang?
- prohibited by your child's school?
- likely to affect your child's employment status?

Getting these issues out on the table will help everyone understand what really matters. **Your interest in your child's well-being becomes the focus of discussion, rather than your embarrassment or judgment of her or him.** Young people are likely to respond to such interest less defensively than they would to the sense that you are simply imposing the orders of the "fashion police."

SAFETY

While most fashion trends are relatively harmless, others can be risky or even dangerous. So the first step in establishing the ground rules for your adolescent's appearance is to **distinguish between legitimate safety concerns and your own social discomfort.**

In general, procedures that involve puncturing the skin (such as piercing and tattooing) carry the risk of infection and, if performed carelessly, transmission of disease. Moreover, such procedures result in more or less permanent alteration of the body. The risk of regret is therefore a serious consideration for adolescents, whose interests and opinions may change rapidly. You may want to set a minimum age at which your child can choose certain styles. For example, you might decide 15 is an acceptable age for ear piercing, but 18 is the minimum age for tattoos or other body piercings. (Or, this type of adornment may simply be unacceptable to you.) Don't wait to talk about such concerns until your child comes to you saying he or she wants a piercing. If you see someone, say, passing your apartment building who has a piercing or tattoo, take that opportunity to discuss the pros and cons of these body adornments.

SELF-ESTEEM

Clothing or makeup that is sexually inappropriate is another safety concern. Clothes that are skintight, skimpy, or otherwise suggestive can put young people at risk for sexual aggression and exploitation. But there is a fine line here. We still want to encourage young people to be proud of their physical appearance and allow them to dress in a way that shows off their favorite features or makes them feel good about themselves. Worry about flesh-revealing clothes may be a reflection of our own discomfort with sexuality. So reflect on your own discomfort, but discuss the situation with your adolescent.

Surging hormones and the bombardment of sexual imagery by the media can combine to pressure young people (especially girls) into dressing for maximum sexual impact. An extreme preoccupation with sexually alluring fashion may indicate that your adolescent has a problem with her self-concept. For example, she may be placing her own worth on her desirability. If you are concerned about this, **be sure to address the issue with great sensitivity**— possibly with the help of a professional counselor.

Young people need nonjudgmental support and encouragement in learning the difference between dressing attractively and dressing provocatively. Make a point of having family discussions about appearance and self-worth. Offer examples of women whose beauty and strength don't rely on scanty attire. Work with your child's school to create a safe, informal setting for youth to talk or write about the role of appearance in self-concept. Emphasize adolescents' positive character traits—honesty, kindness, humor—rather than their appearance.

MOVING TOWARD A POSITIVE IDENTITY

It's possible that despite careful limit-setting and meaningful family discussions, your children will still make choices about their appearance that embarrass or dismay you. At that point, the most important thing you can do is let them know that you love them no matter what they look like. If they are seeking attention through their appearance, be sure they receive the kind of attention they really need and deserve—your loving and respectful regard. Do your best to look past whatever bothers you to recognize and celebrate their genuine inner beauty. Let them know that shaggy or bald, pierced or painted, they are precious to you and nothing they can do will change that.

Even if they dress in ways other than you'd prefer, try to make sure the loudest message you send them goes something like this: "You knew I'd be like what? Although pink hair wouldn't have been my first choice, I think you look great no matter what. I love you, honey. Pink hair and all."

Body Image

Your Dilemma:

"Abby's always asking how she looks in something. 'Mom, does this dress make my butt look too big?' 'Mom, does this sweater make me look fat?'"

or

"Our son is pretty thin. Steve is worried that he's going to be the scrawniest boy in class."

ACTION TIPS

◆ Make it clear to your children that you value them because of who they are, not how they look.

◆ Have family discussions about appearance and how it affects people's self-esteem. Find examples of how the media reinforce unrealistic or unhealthy standards of beauty.

◆ Encourage your children to help others. In addition to making a positive contribution to the community, service to others promotes good self-esteem.

◆ Get help for your son or daughter if necessary. If you're concerned that he or she has an eating disorder or other serious problem related to appearance, don't hesitate to find a counselor or medical professional experienced in working with young people on body-image issues.

◆ Work with your school and community to create youth forums and other opportunities for young people to discuss the role of appearance in their lives.

◆ Have a family cover-up-the-mirrors day.

◆ As a family, make posters of people you admire or who are successful but whose bodies are not mannequin perfect.

WHAT YOUNG PEOPLE SAY: *"I want to feel good about myself."*

"I'm so fat!" If you've ever heard this anguished cry from a rail-thin adolescent, you know that the pressure to conform to certain ideals of beauty can be a very big deal for young people.

Accepting our bodies as they are can be a struggle at any age. It's difficult for any of us to feel at peace with how we look when we're constantly encouraged to feel inadequate by media images of people with "perfect" hair, teeth, skin, figures, and clothes. The pressures of the fashion and entertainment industries find their surest mark among the young, however. For many adolescents, appearance can become a source of great anxiety. And while this problem may be more pronounced in girls, boys are by no means immune.

When young people feel too much emphasis is put on appearance, they may believe they fall short when it comes to a certain standard of beauty, and this can lead to many insecurities. But by encouraging young people to cultivate a strong sense of self-worth, we can help them learn to see beyond the mirror.

The developmental assets are positive qualities, experiences, and skills that children need to grow up healthy and responsible. Parents, grandparents, stepparents, or any other guardian of a child can use these assets as a framework to help them think through the new experiences they're encountering with their children. When dealing with the issue of body image in your family, the assets you may want to consider looking at for guidance are Self-Esteem, Positive Family Communication, Family Support, Service to Others, Positive Peer Influence, Personal Power, Caring School Climate, and Other Adult Relationships.

ASSET TYPE	ASSET NAME	ASSET DESCRIPTION
Positive Identity	Self-Esteem	Young people feel good about themselves.
Support	Positive Family Communication	Young people turn to their parents for advice and support. They have frequent, in-depth conversations with each other on a variety of topics. Parents are approachable and available when their children want to talk.
Support	Family Support	Young people feel loved and supported in their family.
Empowerment	Service to Others	Young people serve in the community one or more hours per week.
Boundaries and Expectations	Positive Peer Influence	Young people's best friends model responsible behavior. They are a good influence. They do well at school and stay away from risky behaviors such as alcohol and other drug use.
Positive Identity	Personal Power	Young people feel that they have control over many things that happen to them.
Support	Caring School Climate	Young people feel that their school supports them, encourages them, and cares about them.
Support	Other Adult Relationships	Young people know other adults besides their parents they can turn to for advice and support. They have frequent, in-depth conversations with them. Ideally, three or more adults play this role in their lives.

SELF-ESTEEM

Communicate to young people that their value is independent of their appearance. **Emphasize character traits and abilities, rather than how attractive they are.** Although an occasional compliment about how nice they look is certainly welcome, excessive emphasis on appearance—even a lot of positive comments—can create a climate in which self-consciousness can grow. Particularly avoid making offhand critical remarks about how an adolescent looks. These may be well-intentioned, but they can have a lingering and destructive effect.

Pay attention to your own attitudes about physical appearance. If you are preoccupied with your own weight or appearance, your children are likely to internalize these attitudes. Try to develop a greater acceptance of how you look, and help your children do the same. This is no small feat, especially given our culture's obsession with youth and beauty. But if you approach body image as something your family can work on together, you may be able to counteract some of the destructive messages.

POSITIVE FAMILY COMMUNICATION

One way to work on body image together is to **have family discussions about the role of appearance and how it affects people's self-esteem.** Look for images in the media that convey positive or negative messages about body image and talk about them. Ask your children their views about how women and men are represented in a particular TV show or movie. Make a list of celebrities who seem overly concerned about their appearance and those who do not. Point out that you can find 15 different types of shampoo, toothpaste, salad dressings, etc. at the store, but magazines and the media emphasize only one body type as the ideal.

Discuss the topic of weight and body image, and ask your children if they feel there is too much emphasis on being thin. See if they think people who are overweight receive the same treatment as those who are thin. Ask them about their own biases and concerns about weight.

FAMILY SUPPORT

Encouraging young people to be physically active is another way to help them develop a healthy body image. Spend time together outdoors as a family—biking, walking, gardening, or tossing a Frisbee around. If you enjoy a particular sport or physical activity, find ways to include your children. Play tennis, soccer, or basketball with them, teach them how to swing dance or do yoga, or ask them to show you dance moves they know. Try a new activity together, such as in-line skating.

Regular exercise, not done to excess, offers countless health benefits. **Emphasize strength and endurance over appearance.** Encourage young people to watch their strength build, for example. How they look can then become less important than being and feeling strong and healthy.

SERVICE TO OTHERS

Perhaps surprisingly, service to others can help young people develop positive attitudes about appearance. **Helping other people is empowering and fosters good self-esteem.** Reaching out to help someone in need also provides perspective on how unimportant appearance actually is. You're less likely to be concerned about how you look when you're helping people who don't have a place to live, for example. And the dog you play with at the Humane Society surely doesn't care whether you have a bumpy nose or the biggest muscles.

Spend time as a family helping others. Encourage your children to get involved in youth programs and organizations that create opportunities for service. Even in small ways, **make helping people part of what your family does.** Offer to shovel the walk for an elderly neighbor. Or, clean up the trash in your local park. Give your children ample opportunities to experience the rewards of giving of themselves.

POSITIVE PEER INFLUENCE

Pay attention to whether your children's friends seem comfortable with their own appearance. **Friends who are overly concerned about clothes, dieting, and other people's appearance can make it difficult for your adolescents to feel at ease about their own bodies.** You may not be able to do a lot about this, however, other than simply being aware of it. Try raising the issue with your children in a nonjudgmental way that conveys your concern about their friends' priorities. Or, see if you can engage their friends in a conversation about appearance and self-esteem. Ask their opinions and listen to what they have to say.

PERSONAL POWER

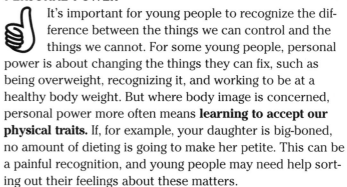

It's important for young people to recognize the difference between the things we can control and the things we cannot. For some young people, personal power is about changing the things they can fix, such as being overweight, recognizing it, and working to be at a healthy body weight. But where body image is concerned, personal power more often means **learning to accept our physical traits.** If, for example, your daughter is big-boned, no amount of dieting is going to make her petite. This can be a painful recognition, and young people may need help sorting out their feelings about these matters.

Young people who are unable to accept themselves as

they are and are unwilling to give up the ideal body image they seek can end up with a distorted image of their own bodies. This can lead to eating disorders and other mental health issues. **If you're concerned that your child is struggling with serious body-image problems, it's extremely important to get professional help right away** from a counselor experienced with eating disorders and related issues. Consult your family physician if you are unsure where to turn for help.

CARING SCHOOL CLIMATE

Ask your children if they feel that too much emphasis is placed on appearance at their school. Do they worry a lot about what to wear and what people might think if their clothes aren't acceptable? Are some students left out or made fun of because of how they look?

Talk to your school's administration and parent association and suggest setting up a discussion group to talk about body-image and self-esteem issues. See if one of the guidance counselors or the school nurse might be willing to hold a discussion over the lunch hour or after school. Find out whether various student leaders might be willing to help educate others about the need to look beyond physical appearance. Maybe someone from a local clinic that deals with eating disorders and other body-image issues would be willing to offer evening talks about the topic. Work with your community to educate other parents and young people about the issue.

OTHER ADULT RELATIONSHIPS

Having other trusted adults in their lives is a great advantage for young people in many respects, and this is certainly true with regard to body image. **If you have a friend or relative who has struggled with self-acceptance and body-image issues, it may be helpful to ask that person to share her or his insights with your children.** Or, perhaps you know someone who is very comfortable "in her or his own skin." Adult role models can help young people find the courage to look beyond appearance and accept themselves as they are.

MIRROR, MIRROR

It's a natural human trait to want to be attractive, and we certainly can't expect young people not to have that desire. But we can help them find balance in their view of themselves so that their inner beauty is as apparent to them as whether their nose is too big or their breasts are too small. We can help them learn to recognize their own genuine worth, so that regardless of how little they conform to a certain beauty ideal, they can look in the mirror and like what they see.

Separation or Divorce

Your Dilemma:

"Lamar wants to know what's going on with me and his mom. He's heard us arguing, but I don't really know how much I should or shouldn't tell him."

or

"My daughter keeps asking me for reassurance. Where do I get my own reassurance that everything's going to be okay?"

ACTION TIPS

◆ Make sure you have enough support from friends, family, and others who care about you. You'll be in better shape to help your children if your own emotional needs are being met.

◆ Give your children plenty of reassurance; let them know you love them, and try to maintain as much continuity as possible in their lives. Keep going to their games and school events, and try to eat meals together as often as possible.

◆ Let your children know you're available to talk anytime. When they do want to talk, be sure to *listen.* Give them your full attention. Remember that you can't "fix" their feelings—you can't make the difficult feelings go away. But you can hear what they have to say and let them know it's important, which is a powerful act of love.

◆ Avoid the temptation to speak harshly about your former or separated spouse to your children, however angry you may be. Find other places to express these feelings—with a friend, a counselor, or in a journal. You'll spare your children a lot of unnecessary pain and confusion if you don't put them in the middle.

◆ Try to help your adolescents develop supportive relationships with other trusted adults. Talk to friends, relatives, school counselors, neighbors, and people at your place of worship who care about your family. Ask them to make contact with your children and show their interest and concern.

◆ Encourage your children to continue to explore their interests and take care of themselves. Resist the temptation to have them take care of you.

FACT: Forty-five percent of all American children can expect their families to break up before they reach the age of 18.

From: *Issues in Ethics* Vol. 9, Num. 5, Spring 1998

One of the most difficult aspects of parenting is that you're often called upon to help and comfort your children when you feel least capable of doing so. At such times, what you may really want is someone to assist and care for you.

This challenge is seldom more painful than when you're going through a separation or divorce. The strain and emotional trauma of separation and divorce can leave you feeling exhausted, confused, angry, scared, heartbroken, and depressed—sometimes all at once. If the situation is particularly ugly, you're likely to feel even worse. With accusations flying and nasty remarks poisoning the air, the home you once shared can take on the atmosphere of a hostile planet.

In the midst of all that, you may suddenly look into your adolescent's worried face and feel the last trace of your composure crumble. The pain written there is plain to see. Where on earth are you going to find the strength to offer comfort and reassurance? How can you guide and support your children when you've never felt so lost in your life? Where can you turn for help?

The developmental assets are positive qualities, experiences, and skills that children need to grow up healthy and responsible. Parents, grandparents, stepparents, or any other guardian of a child can use these assets as a framework to help them think through the new experiences they're encountering with their children. When dealing with the issue of separation or divorce in your family, the assets or asset categories you may want to consider looking at for guidance are Support, Self-Esteem, Family Support, Positive Family Communication, Interpersonal Competence, and Other Adult Relationships.

ASSET TYPE	ASSET NAME	ASSET DESCRIPTION
Support	Asset #1 Family Support Asset #2 Positive Family Communication Asset #3 Other Adult Relationships Asset #4 Caring Neighborhood Asset #5 Caring School Climate Asset #6 Parent Involvement in Schooling	Young people need to experience support, care, and love from their families and many others. They need organizations and institutions that provide positive, supportive environments.
Positive Identity	Self-Esteem	Young people feel good about themselves.
Support	Family Support	Young people feel loved and supported in their family.
Support	Positive Family Communication	Young people turn to their parents for advice and support. They have frequent, in-depth conversations with each other on a variety of topics. Parents are approachable and available when their children want to talk.
Social Competencies	Interpersonal Competence	Young people have empathy, sensitivity, and friendship skills.
Support	Other Adult Relationships	Young people know other adults besides their parents they can turn to for advice and support. They have frequent, in-depth conversations with them. Ideally, three or more adults play this role in their lives.

SUPPORT

You can't do this alone. **Take a careful look at your support network.** Is it enough? Do you have people you can count on to help you get through this? If so, don't be afraid to lean on them—or to let them know how much you appreciate them. Call them when you need help, when you need to talk, when you need to hear a friendly voice. Let them remind you what a good person you are and that there are a lot of people who love you.

If, on the other hand, you find your safety net is looking pretty small, **start reaching out.** You need someone to talk to about what you're going through—other than your children. Join a support group for people going through divorce. There are many community resources, support groups, and counselors that can help you. Talking with others in a similar situation can be reassuring and can also provide a fertile ground in which new friendships can blossom. If problems feel bigger, however, don't hesitate to seek professional help. Going to counseling or therapy is a sign that you value your emotional health.

Take a chance with someone you don't know very well. If there's a neighbor who's always seemed friendly, invite her or him out for coffee, not necessarily to talk about your problems, but just to start making connections. Or, get to know the parents of one of your child's friends.

Be open to surprises. Sometimes help comes from unexpected quarters. An old friend may call you from out of the blue and want to get together. Or, someone you thought seemed distant and aloof turns out to be in a situation similar to yours, and you find you have a lot in common.

SELF-ESTEEM

Divorce can wreak havoc on your self-concept, so **take extra care of yourself** during this time. Get as much rest and exercise as you can, eat well, and spend time with the people you love, who make you laugh, or who make you feel good about yourself. Make a point of getting out and having fun once in awhile. Try something new—take a class, change your hairstyle, rearrange your furniture. If you're healthy and rested and able to laugh, you'll be in a much better position to help your children cope with the changes at home. And when a young person sees that a caregiver is taking care of her- or himself, this relieves the adolescent from feeling like he or she has to take care of the adult.

During this time, your children may be feeling bad about themselves, too. They may even feel as if the separation or divorce is their fault. **Reassure them that they are not to blame for this situation,** and try to do what you can to boost their self-esteem. Express your love for your children

regularly. Every day, tell them how much they mean to you. Let your children know what makes you proud of them. Make a list of their best qualities. All of these reminders let your children know they are good people.

FAMILY SUPPORT

Adolescents may put on a brave face, but there's no question that divorce is hard on children of any age. **They need plenty of reassurance;** they need to know the world isn't falling apart, even if it might feel that way sometimes. And it's very important that they know they still have two parents who love them. Above all, they need reassurance that they are not to blame.

As much as possible, try to **maintain familiar routines.** Keep going to their basketball games, even if you feel like staying away because you don't want to run into someone who might ask how you're doing. Avoid the tendency to become isolated. As often as you can, try to have at least one meal together on the days you're with your children. Keep in touch with them, and ask how they're doing.

Encourage young people to continue to explore their own interests and take care of themselves. Resist the temptation to have them take care of you. This is an important time of self-discovery in their lives that requires their energy and your support, even as you shore up your own.

There are great books out there written by young people for children whose parents divorce. Get some at the library or bookstore for your adolescent.

POSITIVE FAMILY COMMUNICATION

Make sure you hear what your children tell you. One of the most important things you can do for your children (and this is true any time, not just during divorce) is to **listen to them.** Listen deeply, with your full attention. And—here's the hard part—don't try to fix anything. Don't try to "make it better" or cheer them up. If they're angry, let them be angry. If they're sad, let them be sad. You don't have to take the blame or deflect the blame; you don't have to talk them into or out of anything. Just listen, really *listen,* to what they have to say.

This doesn't mean you should be indifferent. Far from it. Let them know you love them, let them know you care about how they feel, **but just let them *feel* what they feel.** It's okay. There's nothing inherently damaging about feeling angry or upset. The feelings are just there, and they'll eventually go away. By simply acknowledging the importance of whatever emotion is predominant at the moment, you help your children trust what they feel. You also help them trust their ability to express their emotions. In doing so, it becomes much easier for them to let go of their feelings and move on.

INTERPERSONAL COMPETENCE

On the one hand, your children need to hear that this time is difficult for you, too, and that you are taking care of yourself and getting the help you need. On the other hand, they shouldn't be exposed to all the details of your struggle, which is one reason it's so important for you to have other people to talk to about what's going on. **Sharing your own feelings with your children about what's happening to your family requires a lot of sensitivity and restraint.**

It's especially important to **avoid talking to them in a disparaging or angry way about your spouse** (or ex). Research shows that young people do best when parent relationships are friendly and healthy. It may be tempting to snipe, particularly if you're the subject of unkind remarks from the other side. Even saying, "Oh, he's late again," puts your ex in a negative light in your children's eyes. You'll spare them a lot of unnecessary pain and turmoil if you keep these thoughts to yourself. (Try keeping an "anger journal" or venting these feelings with a friend instead.) You'll also keep the lines of communication between you and your children open. They may not feel able to come to you with certain problems if they think you're going to criticize the other parent.

Keep in mind your ex may be one of your child's best friends. If your child comes to you with a problem about the other parent, it's okay to acknowledge the situation, but try to emphasize the positive. You might say, "I understand what you're saying. I've experienced similar concerns and frustrations, but your father/mother has many wonderful qualities and I'm sure he/she loves you very much."

OTHER ADULT RELATIONSHIPS

In whatever way you can, **try to keep your child in touch with other caring adults** during this time.

Aunts and uncles, friends and neighbors can all be extremely helpful in providing a sympathetic ear and a sense of continuity and stability.

Consider talking to the guidance counselor or a trusted teacher at your adolescent's school about the difficulties he or she is experiencing at home. It can be helpful for someone at school to have this information, so they can make a special point of checking in with your child informally.

If you belong to a congregation or other supportive network, **seek help from others who have gone through divorce.** You might look into finding or creating a support group for adolescents whose parents are divorced. Hearing what other young people are going through and having a place to talk can be a great help.

A POSITIVE FUTURE

There's no getting around the fact that divorce, especially when children are involved, is a wrenching experience. But there are things you can do to ease the pain. Draw strength and support wherever you can find it, and pass it along to your children. Seeing you face this hardship with courage and grace will let them know that you are doing your best to help make sure that things really will get better.

Single Parenting

Your Dilemma:

**"Driving, cooking, cleaning, listening, understanding. I have to do everything.
Sometimes it gets to be too much."**

or

**"I feel like I don't have time to do enough for my children.
I feel like I'm not a good parent."**

ACTION TIPS

◆ Work on building your support network. Join a parenting support group. Ask trusted friends to spend time with your child. Get to know your neighbors so you have people to turn to when you need help—and your child does, too.

◆ Take care of yourself. Getting regular exercise, eating well, and getting enough sleep can make a big difference in how well you can cope with the demands of parenting.

◆ Learn to recognize when you need a break—and take one. Even getting away for a short time can lift your spirits and renew your energy.

◆ Cut yourself some slack. Think about all the things you do right as a parent. Give yourself the reassurance you would give a dear friend who was in your situation. Treat yourself with kindness and respect.

FACT: "While there are certainly no perfect parents, the vast majority of parents meet their children's basic needs and contribute significantly—more than anyone else— to their children's healthy growth and development."

From: *Building Strong Families* a report by YMCA and Search Institute

The hardest thing (and there are many hard things) about being a single parent is not the lack of free time, or the abundance of bills, or even the fact that your boss is getting a little tired of how many sick days you've been taking to tend to your children. What's hardest about being a single parent is that everything—and we're talking *every*-thing—is up to you.

Every doctor's appointment, piano lesson, school conference, soccer game, trip to the emergency room, I-forgot-about-my-science-project-and-I-have-to-get-supplies situation. Every wardrobe crisis. *("I need a new shirt for the concert—by tomorrow!")* Every transportation crisis. *("Allison was supposed to pick me up, but she has a flat tire. Can you come get me?")* Every social crisis. *("Adam told Ling I said she was fat. Now everyone hates me.")* Every lunch that has to be made and every field-trip consent form that has to be turned in. Every decision about your adolescents' daily life, health, discipline, education, future, and over-all well-being. It all comes down to you. No wonder you feel tired and overwhelmed.

Of course, every parent feels that way some-times, even those who have energetic and commit-ted partners. Parenting is an extremely demanding job with enormous responsibilities. But at least parents with partners have someone else to take up some of the slack. Theoretically, at least, they can offer support and encouragement. They can discuss the dozens of large and small decisions that parents make every day, and they can share responsibility for how things are going.

The developmental assets are positive quali-ties, experiences, and skills that children need to grow up healthy and responsible. Parents, grand-parents, stepparents, or any other guardian of a child can use these assets as a framework to help them think through the new experiences they're encountering with their children. When dealing with the issue of single parenting in your family, the assets and larger asset categories you may want to consider looking at for guidance are Support, Youth as Resources, Personal Power, and Self-Esteem.

ASSET TYPE	ASSET NAME	ASSET DESCRIPTION
Support	Asset #1 Family Support Asset #2 Positive Family Communication Asset #3 Other Adult Relationships Asset #4 Caring Neighborhood Asset #5 Caring School Climate Asset #6 Parent Involvement in Schooling	Young people need to experience support, care, and love from their families and many others. They need organizations and institutions that provide positive, supportive environments.
Empowerment	Youth as Resources	Young people are given useful roles in the community.
Positive Identity	Personal Power	Young people feel that they have control over many things that happen to them.
Positive Identity	Self-Esteem	Young people feel good about themselves.

SUPPORT

We all need backup—we just can't do everything ourselves. So if we don't have it, we have to create it. Here are a few ideas for getting more support for yourself and for your children.

Join a support group. If there's a parent support group in your area specifically for single parents of adolescents, all the better. If you can't find a group that works for you, start one—maybe you can do a brown-bag lunch with others in your same situation. Arrange to get together regularly with other parents to share stories and concerns and to give each other encouragement and support. Ask for help from your local school or congregation if you have trouble getting a group started. Having other parents to talk to helps reduce the sense of isolation that is often part of single parenting.

Help your child find a mentor. This might be a trusted neighbor or friend, someone from your congregation who shares a common interest with your child, or a caring teacher. Meet with this person and discuss the important role of caring adults in young people's lives. Ask if he or she would be willing to make a short-term commitment, say six months, to spending time with your son or daughter on a regular basis. Keeping it within a certain time frame can make it feel more manageable for the mentor but leave the possibility open that it could grow into a lasting relationship.

Call on your friends. Ask the people who care about you and your child to help out in specific, concrete ways. For example, if your best friend is good at building things, maybe she can help your daughter build some shelves in her room. Or, if another friend or relative is an artist, maybe he can help your son with his art project. Invite a friend to your child's performance or game. Or, ask a friend to take your child out to lunch or a movie. The important thing is for children of all ages to know that there are a number of adults who care about them. Keep a calendar, and try to schedule at least one such event each month with various friends and family members.

Participate in neighborhood and other social events where you can find support. The stress you feel from single parenting may make you feel like withdrawing and isolating yourself. Instead, try to reach out and encourage your children and yourself to stay engaged in constructive activities.

Get to know your neighbors. Introduce your adolescents to everyone, and get to know as many of the other young people by name as you can. Talk to other parents and adults about watching out for everyone's safety. Exchange phone numbers, and add those persons with whom you're comfortable to your family's list of emergency contacts.

Encourage young people to help out in the neighborhood. Make it a family project to help an elderly or shut-in neighbor with lawn care or shopping. Do a neighborhood litter cleanup together. Ask your children to help make a meal for neighbors who are bereaved. Getting young people involved in the neighborhood strengthens their ties to the community in ways that benefit everyone.

Be sure you have plenty of people to turn to for help. Get to know the parents of your children's friends. If you're feeling overwhelmed, don't hesitate to seek the help of a counselor or therapist. Getting professional help is a sign that you value your emotional health.

YOUTH AS RESOURCES

 Find appropriate ways to share responsibility with your adolescent. Not only does it help to get things done, but also it shows that they're valued. You can also enjoy doing tasks together. However, don't fall into the trap of expecting your adolescent to become the "adult" in the family.

PERSONAL POWER

In the constant effort to keep everyone fed, clothed, sheltered, nurtured, and safe, it's easy to forget that you need care, too. It's important for all parents to remember to take time for themselves, but especially so for single parents, whose needs can easily get lost in the shuffle. The bind, of course, is that **if you don't get what you need, your children don't get what they need either because you'll be stressed out and exhausted.** Here are a few suggestions for keeping life more balanced:

- **Schedule some time each week that's just for you.** Visit a museum, go for a hike, have lunch with a friend, read a book, or take a long soak in the tub. However you choose to spend the time, really let yourself relax and enjoy it. You deserve it.

- **Make a point of eating well, getting regular exercise, and getting enough sleep.** Taking good care of your body will help you have more energy and resilience.

- **Try to arrange a true getaway once in awhile.** Ask a friend or relative to stay with your children for the weekend, and go do something fun.

- **Develop a strong support network.** Spend time with friends who make you happy; limit the time you spend with people who drain your energy. Remember that friendships need time and attention. Make the effort to include your friends in your life and in your children's lives. It's important for young people to see that friendship is important to you.

SELF-ESTEEM

You have a tough job, maybe the toughest job there is. **Give yourself credit for the things you're doing well,** and cut yourself some slack about the things that need work. If you're stressed out and you snap at your child, recognize this as a signal that you need a break—and be sure that you get one. Call a friend, rent a funny movie, or go for a walk. Try to step back and see the big picture, and be sure to apologize and agree to move on.

Above all, be kind to yourself. **Recognize that you don't have to do everything perfectly,** that you get to make mistakes. Learn to view yourself with the same generosity that you might reserve for a dear friend. If you can relax and accept yourself as you are, your children will learn to do the same. It's so easy to get caught up in the frantic struggle to give our young people everything they need; we tend to forget that one of the best gifts we can give them is our own happiness.

SINGLE, BUT NOT ALONE

Being a parent is demanding; being a single parent is especially so. By making sure we get our own needs met and by working to build a strong network of support for ourselves and our children, we can help ensure that our family has what it needs to flourish.

Finding Other Adults

Other Adult Relationships (Asset #3) is part of the Support category. Here are some ideas for programs and opportunities where you can look for safe adults to spend meaningful time with your children.

- Neighborhood get-togethers
- Religious programs
- Music lessons
- Sports leagues
- Community recreation
- Internships
- Family reunions and gatherings
- Kinship programs
- Tutoring
- Theater projects
- Youth groups
- Hobby classes
- Community bands, orchestras, and choirs
- Camps
- Mentoring
- Service-learning programs in schools

You can also talk with your children. Ask questions such as:

- Which adult besides me would you like to get to know better? Why?
- Which adults in your life do you respect, admire, or trust—or might if you could get to know them better?
- If you had a tough question that you didn't want to discuss with me, to whom would you go or to whom do you wish you could go?
- What adult would you like to talk to if you wanted to talk about dating and relationships?
- What adult would you like to talk to about what to do after graduation?

Race and Ethnicity

Your Dilemma:

"Our neighborhood isn't very diverse. I'd like Ian to be comfortable around people of backgrounds different from our own."

or

"I don't think Maria appreciates her ethnic heritage."

ACTION TIPS

◆ Find different ways to discuss the topic of race in your family. For example, read a book together and talk about the racial implications. Celebrate Martin Luther King, Jr. Day as a family. Talk about the racial roles and stereotypes you see in the media.

◆ Help your son or daughter look for ways to get actively involved in social change. Ideas include volunteering as a family at an organization whose goals you admire or getting young people involved in setting up a community discussion about race and culture.

◆ Encourage your child to have friends from diverse cultures.

◆ Serve dinners with dishes from other cultures, and in family celebrations, include traditions from other cultures.

◆ Encourage your children to take a stand and speak up if they feel they have been discriminated against or if they see that someone else has.

WHAT YOUNG PEOPLE SAY: "Teach acceptance, respect, and the balance between individuality/group interdependence right from the beginning, and you won't have to teach tolerance."

Regardless of your own racial and cultural heritage—whether you're Native American, Asian, African American, Arab, Hispanic, or white—race is an undeniable reality of modern life. Race influences where we live, where we work, where we go to school, what kind of opportunities we have, who our friends are, and how we perceive the world and the people in it.

Our attitudes and beliefs about race and culture become part of the bundle of values we pass along to our children. Therefore, it's important to examine them carefully and make sure they are worthy of being handed down. Our children carry into the world the sense of responsibility and morals we model for them. One of the greatest

gifts we can give them is the belief in their own ability to help create a truly fair and equal society.

The developmental assets are positive qualities, experiences, and skills that children need to grow up healthy and responsible. Parents, grandparents, stepparents, or any other guardian of a child can use these assets as a framework to help them think through the new experiences they're encountering with their children. When dealing with the issue of race and ethnicity in your family, the assets you may want to consider looking at for guidance are Positive Family Communication, Equality and Social Justice, Cultural Competence, and Integrity.

ASSET TYPE	ASSET NAME	ASSET DESCRIPTION
Support	Positive Family Communication	Young people turn to their parents for advice and support. They have frequent, in-depth conversations with each other on a variety of topics. Parents are approachable and available when their children want to talk.
Positive Values	Equality and Social Justice	Young people place high value on promoting equality and reducing hunger and poverty.
Social Competencies	Cultural Competence	Young people know and are comfortable with people of different cultural, racial, and/or ethnic backgrounds.
Positive Values	Integrity	Young people act on their convictions and stand up for their beliefs.

POSITIVE FAMILY COMMUNICATION

When young people learn to discuss racism and social justice openly in a safe setting, they're better prepared to confront these issues when they arise in the world outside. In your family discussions of racial issues, be honest about your own feelings, but make a point to create an atmosphere of tolerance so that everyone can speak freely. The following are some ideas for stimulating the discussion:

- **Choose a book to read together that deals with race,** such as *The Adventures of Huckleberry Finn* by Mark Twain or *Through My Eyes* by Ruby Bridges and discuss the issues it raises.

- **Celebrate Martin Luther King, Jr. Day with your family.** Check out library tapes of Dr. King's speeches. Listen to them together and talk about their emotional impact, the ideas he put forth, and the effects of the work he did. Or, participate in community events that commemorate his life and work.

- **Talk about racial roles and stereotypes as they're depicted in movies and TV shows.** Help your children identify stereotypes and make a commitment not to use them in your family. Talk about ways to respond when others voice stereotypes to you. Together, make a list of stories that portray people of color as multidimensional human beings and contrast them to those whose portrayals are narrow or demeaning.

- **Start a "Person of the Month" award in your family.** Take turns nominating someone who is doing important work for social justice, and then have a family vote. The candidates might be people you know, such as teachers or fellow students, or prominent figures working at the national or international level. Post a picture of the current winner in your home, and share information about the person's activities. Write a letter as a family telling the recipients about the award and thanking them for their good work.

- **Obtain resources, such as books or videos, that provide you and your adolescents with the perspectives of people of cultures different from your own.**

- **List and explore the barriers that exist for certain groups of people from nonmajority cultures.**

EQUALITY AND SOCIAL JUSTICE

Young people can take an active role in bringing about positive change in the world. Their efforts will not only benefit their school or community, but will also foster a personal sense of satisfaction and self-respect. Here are some ways to help young people reach out into the community and make a difference:

- **Select an organization that promotes equality and social justice and as a family, support its efforts.** Young people can contribute part of their allowance or earnings to the cause. Consider making a family contribution to such an organization instead of spending money on holiday gifts. If money is short, send a letter to the organization expressing your family's support.

- **If race is a particularly explosive issue in your community or in your adolescent's school or life, get involved in working to resolve the problem.** Work with the school administration to help young people start a campaign for peace. Help create leadership roles for young people in conflict resolution. Enlist the help of community leaders and local media to make others in the community aware of the problem. Look for ways to make sure your children have a voice in matters of interest to them and insist that all groups have a voice.

- **Sponsor a community discussion about racial or cultural issues, and include students in planning the event.** Give them key roles in facilitating the discussion, and be sure their concerns get heard and addressed. Identify problem situations in the community, and brainstorm possible solutions. Create an action team that includes young people to implement the ideas, and follow up with another meeting to report the results to the community.

CULTURAL COMPETENCE

The more young people know about different races and cultures, the more comfortable they will be in all kinds of situations.

- **Talk about your family's cultural background and experiences and how they have affected your lives.** Having a positive view of their own racial or ethnic group can give your children a more positive view of other groups.

- **Participate, as a family, in events and activities that celebrate various cultures and religions.** Discuss these experiences and share what you learn.

- **In family celebrations, include traditions from different cultures.**

INTEGRITY

Unfortunately, discrimination based on race and ethnicity, as well as many other factors, such as age, gender, sexual orientation, and religion, takes place every day. **We can help our children learn to handle such discrimination with dignity by encouraging them to stand up for themselves and tell someone if they think they have been discriminated against.** If telling someone, such as a person in charge, doesn't work, they may want to try writing a letter to the local newspaper. Your children can ask themselves questions if they believe they have been treated unfairly. How did they compare to others who had the same goal they had? On what was the outcome based—experience, attitude, ability, or education? Or, was the outcome based on race, religion, sex, or age? Answering these questions can help them determine if they have been discriminated against.

A CARING WORLD

Racism and social injustice still cause tremendous suffering in the world. As citizens, we have a responsibility to remedy this situation in whatever way we can. And as caregivers, we have a responsibility to teach our children to do the same.

As the lives of great leaders and citizens such as Mahatma Gandhi, Martin Luther King, Jr., Rosa Parks, and Nelson Mandela attest, brave and dedicated people can alter the course of history. In our own lives, we can make a commitment to working for equality and social justice, and we can teach our children the importance of upholding these principles. Such courage is our greatest gift.

DID YOU KNOW?

According to one survey, African American parents are more likely than white parents to say they daily teach their child to get along with people of different races or backgrounds.

From: *Building Strong Families* a report by YMCA and Search Institute

---

Rate Your Cultural Competence

You and your children can rate yourselves on the following score sheet. Use your answers as a tool for discussion to figure out ways to increase your cultural competence.

TYPE OF CONTACT	WEEKLY	MONTHLY	YEARLY	RARELY	NEVER
1. I see people from a variety of cultural backgrounds in my neighborhood.					
2. I see people from a variety of cultural backgrounds in my community.					
3. I talk to people with cultural backgrounds different from mine.					
4. I watch TV shows that positively portray people from a variety of cultural backgrounds.					
5. I listen to music from cultures other than my own.					
6. I hear others talk positively about people from a variety of cultures.					
7. I eat foods from cultures other than my own.					
8. I study in school about people with a variety of cultural backgrounds.					
9. I read positive stories about people from many different cultures.					
10. I attend cross-cultural events.					

Substance Abuse

Your Dilemma:

**"We want to talk to Toby about drugs and drinking, but we also
want him to know that we trust him."**

or

**"Faye has been avoiding us lately, and she won't go on family outings anymore.
She doesn't seem like herself. We're worried that she
might be using drugs."**

ACTION TIPS

◆ Be clear about your expectations regarding alcohol and other drugs and communicate them to your children. Expect young people to succeed, and accept them when they don't.

◆ Talk about drinking and other drug use in your family discussions. Give your children opportunities to express their own views on the subject.

◆ Get help if you suspect your child has a substance abuse problem. Talk to her or his school's guidance counselor or a family therapist, or contact a treatment facility or 12-step program.

◆ Model restraint in your own life. If you drink, use moderation. If you're concerned about your own substance use, get professional help.

◆ Help your children develop meaningful friendships with other trusted adults. Encourage them to get involved in activities that offer them contact with caring adults.

◆ Be honest about your own past drug use if asked by your adolescents and tell them what you learned from your experience.

WHAT YOUNG PEOPLE SAY: "Accept and understand my mistakes."

For many parents, talking to their children about alcohol and other drugs can be an emotionally charged experience. Some parents refuse to believe that their children would ever drink or use other drugs, even when the evidence clearly points in that direction. Other parents who grew up in the '60s and '70s feel hypocritical telling their children not to do things they themselves did in their youth. Still others find the topic so upsetting that they don't want to discuss it at all.

Yet young people need a great deal of guidance and support in this area. Substance abuse among adolescents is a significant problem, and the consequences can be serious. With the help of a loving family and supportive community, however, young people can be supported in making wise choices.

The developmental assets are positive qualities, experiences, and skills that children need to grow up healthy and responsible. Parents, grandparents, stepparents, or any other guardian of a child can use these assets as a framework to help them think through the new experiences they're encountering with their children. When dealing with the issue of substance abuse in your family, the assets and asset categories you may want to consider looking at for guidance are Positive Peer Influence, High Expectations, Family Boundaries, Positive Family Communication, Support, Restraint, Resistance Skills, Other Adult Relationships, and Creative Activities.

ASSET TYPE	ASSET NAME	ASSET DESCRIPTION
Boundaries and Expectations	Positive Peer Influence	Young people's best friends model responsible behavior. They are a good influence. They do well at school and stay away from risky behaviors such as alcohol and other drug use.
Boundaries and Expectations	High Expectations	Parents and teachers encourage young people to do well.
Boundaries and Expectations	Family Boundaries	Parents set clear rules and consequences for their children's behavior. They monitor their children's whereabouts.
Support	Positive Family Communication	Young people turn to their parents for advice and support. They have frequent, in-depth conversations with each other on a variety of topics. Parents are approachable and available when their children want to talk.
Support	Asset #1 Family Support Asset #2 Positive Family Communication Asset #3 Other Adult Relationships Asset #4 Caring Neighborhood Asset #5 Caring School Climate Asset #6 Parent Involvement in Schooling	Young people need to experience support, care, and love from their families and many others. They need organizations and institutions that provide positive, supportive environments.

(continued)

ASSET TYPE	ASSET NAME	ASSET DESCRIPTION
Positive Values	Restraint	Young people believe that it's important not to be sexually active or to use alcohol or other drugs.
Social Competencies	Resistance Skills	Young people can resist negative peer pressure and avoid dangerous situations.
Support	Other Adult Relationships	Young people know other adults besides their parents they can turn to for advice and support. They have frequent, in-depth conversations with them. Ideally, three or more adults play this role in their lives.
Constructive Use of Time	Creative Activities	Young people spend three or more hours each week in lessons or practice in music, theater, or other arts.

POSITIVE PEER INFLUENCE

Research strongly suggests that peer influence affects substance abuse. **Get to know your children's friends, and pay attention to the friends they spend time with.** Talk to them about their interests, ask their opinions on various topics, and be open to their ideas. Try to look beyond appearances and learn to appreciate them for who they are.

Encourage positive and supportive friendships. For example, if you notice that certain friends have a positive effect on your children, say so: "You always seem happy when Sarah's around." On the other hand, if you're concerned that certain friendships seem unhealthy or conducive to risky behaviors, express those concerns to your children, too. Consider setting some limits on the amount of contact your children have with friends who seem to bring out negative attitudes and behaviors in them. Keep in mind, however, that such restrictions are likely to cause conflict and should not be entered into lightly.

HIGH EXPECTATIONS

Young people do best when we expect their best from them. Make it clear what you expect from your adolescents with respect to avoiding alcohol or other drugs. For example, you might simply tell them you expect them not to drink or use drugs while they are adolescents. **For many young people, having clear expectations gives them the strength they need to resist negative peer pressure.**

Frame your expectations in positive terms. **Let your children know that you believe in them and that you trust them to make good choices.** When they make mistakes, which is a natural part of learning and growing, let them know you're disappointed in their *choices*, but make it clear that your love for them is undiminished.

Changes in your child's typical behavior patterns could be the indication of a substance abuse problem. Possible distress signals include cutting classes, staying out past curfew, doing poorly in school, abandoning old friends for a new crowd, lying, or becoming withdrawn, moody, or unusually aggressive.

FAMILY BOUNDARIES

Establish clear boundaries and consequences related to alcohol and other drug use. Loss of certain privileges may be an appropriate consequence for a single incident of smoking marijuana or drinking alcohol. (For example, you might take away driving privileges or the freedom to go to parties with a certain group of friends.) Even a seemingly isolated incident calls for a lot of discussion and careful inquiry. It's both an important signal

that something may be wrong in a young person's world, and a valuable opportunity to get her or his life back on track.

Repeated incidents involving alcohol or other drug use, or concerns about friends who are using drugs, should cause everyone who cares about the young person to have a serious response. Talk to a counselor or other professional to learn about the best way to approach the subject with your child.

POSITIVE FAMILY COMMUNICATION

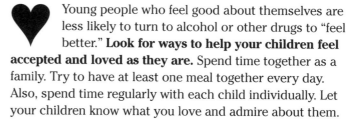
Be sure your adolescents know that you're available to talk. If you're busy with something else, let them know when you'll be done and then seek them out to follow up. Don't wait for them to bring it up again.

Include the topic of alcohol and other drug use among regular family discussions. Ask your children about their views on the subject, and listen to what they have to say. Share your concerns. If you find the topic hard to talk about, ask advice from your school's guidance counselor, your family doctor, or a therapist who works with young people.

Drug use affects communication. A child who is using drugs is likely to withdraw from family interaction. If you notice your child avoiding family discussions and activities, express your concerns directly; put extra effort into including her or him, and consider seeking professional help.

If you suspect your child is using drugs: **Make an effort to talk about it calmly.** If you're feeling particularly angry or upset, wait a day or so to broach the subject. Keep in mind that it's very important at this point to keep the communication channels open. Make it clear that you disapprove of the choices, not the child. Restate your expectations, and let your child know that you believe in her or his ability to make better choices in the future. State that you will support and assist your child as he or she makes healthy choices.

SUPPORT

Young people who feel good about themselves are less likely to turn to alcohol or other drugs to "feel better." **Look for ways to help your children feel accepted and loved as they are.** Spend time together as a family. Try to have at least one meal together every day. Also, spend time regularly with each child individually. Let your children know what you love and admire about them. Take an interest in their friends, their school, their ideas, and their dreams.

If you think your child may have a substance abuse problem: **Get help from as many sources as possible.** Don't try to cope with the situation alone or keep it a secret within your family. Don't let feelings of embarrassment keep you from getting the help you need. Gather information from

12-step groups, such as Alcoholics Anonymous (AA) or Narcotics Anonymous (NA), or from a drug-treatment program in your area. Enlist the help of supportive friends, relatives, caring teachers, and school counselors. Learn more through a visit to the library. If you belong to a place of worship, seek the help of people in your congregation who have dealt with substance abuse in their own lives.

If your child is struggling with substance abuse: **All young people need to know they are loved and supported, but an adolescent who is grappling with substance abuse needs a tremendous amount of reassurance.** Be affectionate and let your love for your child guide your actions and your words. Spend time together doing things you both enjoy, such as going to a movie or working in the garden. Allow conversations to arise naturally; don't feel you have to bring up "the problem" whenever you spend time together.

Be sure *you* have adequate support from friends and loved ones. **Getting your own emotional needs met will help you be more resilient in coping with this situation.** It's a good idea to have a therapist, counselor, or clergy person to talk to about what your family is going through.

RESTRAINT AND RESISTANCE SKILLS

  Help your child develop an understanding of the importance of restraint. **Be clear about your own views on this subject, and teach and model restraint in your own life.** If you drink, for example, use moderation. If you have concerns about your own substance use, get help. Look for examples in movies and TV shows of people demonstrating restraint, and discuss these with your children.

Work with young people on developing resistance skills in social situations. Brainstorm or role play ways to handle negative peer pressure. Emphasize the importance of making their own intentions clear in such situations; if they're clear about what they want, people will take them seriously. Offer examples of negative peer pressure from your own experience, and talk about what enters into your own decisions about using alcohol and other drugs.

OTHER ADULT RELATIONSHIPS

Having a number of trusted adults to talk to and spend time with is extremely beneficial for young people. **Try to help your children establish friendships with other caring adults.** Find out if their school offers a mentoring program, or talk to people in your religious community to see if you might be able to find a trusted adult friend for your children there. Encourage your adolescents to get involved in youth programs in the community, such as 4H, YMCA, or Camp Fire USA activities, which bring them in contact with caring adults.

If your child has a substance abuse problem: **Friendships with trusted adults are a great source of support for young people who are trying to deal with substance abuse.** An adult friend who has dealt with substance abuse in her or his own life can be especially helpful. Programs such as Alcoholics Anonymous or Narcotics Anonymous, which build on a relationship with a guiding "sponsor," can be one way for your son or daughter to establish such a connection.

CREATIVE ACTIVITIES

 Many people turn to alcohol and other drugs as a way to avoid painful feelings. Help your children find creative outlets for the intense emotions that can sometimes make adolescence turbulent. Artistic expression can be extremely valuable for young people, giving them a way to transform difficult feelings into something meaningful and life-affirming. Encourage your children to write, draw, or paint. Find out about music or drama programs and opportunities at their school, in your congregation, or in the community. Share your own creative interests with your children, and think of artistic projects you can work on together.

DID YOU KNOW?

The more assets young people have, the less likely they are to turn to alcohol and other drugs—and the more likely they are to choose life circumstances that allow them to thrive.

From: Search Institute

ALIVE AND THRIVING

Helping young people steer clear of alcohol and other drug use and abuse involves more than simply warning them about the dangers. It involves helping them create conditions in which they feel safe, supported, and free to talk about whatever is on their mind. Young people who can easily think of 10 people who love them and want the best for them are on firmer ground than those who can't. We can help the young people in our lives avoid the pitfalls and find their own true path by making sure they have abundant love and support along the way.

---

25 Ways to Resist Negative Peer Pressure

Resistance skills are key to helping young people avoid the dangers of substance use and abuse. You may want to gather as a family and discuss the following negative-peer-pressure resistance techniques.

1. Walk away.

2. Ignore the person.

3. Pretend the person must be joking. ("What a riot! You are so funny.")

4. Say no—calmly but firmly.

5. Say no and give a reason. ("No. Cigarette smoke makes me sick.")

6. Say no and state a value or belief that's important to you. ("No. I've decided not to drink until I turn the legal age.")

7. Say no and warn about the possible consequences. ("No way! We could all get expelled.")

8. Say no and change the subject. ("No, I'm not interested. Say, what did you think of that joke Clarisse made in math class today?")

9. Say no and offer a positive alternative. ("No, thanks. I'll pass. I'm going for a bike ride. Want to come?")

10. Say no and ask a question. ("No! Why would I want to do that?")

11. Say no and use humor. ("Forget it. I'd rather go play on the freeway. It's safer.")

12. Say no and apply some pressure of your own. ("No. Say, I always thought you were smarter than that.")

13. Share your feelings. ("I don't like being around people who are drinking.")

14. Use your parents as an excuse. ("My dad would kill me if I ever did that.")

15. Stick up for yourself. ("I'm not going to do that. It wouldn't be good for me.")

16. Confront the person. ("I can't believe you'd ask me to do that. I thought you were my friend.")

17. Call another friend to help you.

18. Always have an out—a plan B. ("Sorry, I can't come to the party. I promised my sister I'd take her to a movie.")

19. Lie. ("Gotta run. I told my mom I'd clean out the garage.")

20. Laugh.

21. Hang out with people who don't pressure you to do risky things.

22. Ask a peer mediator to help.

23. Tell an adult.

24. Trust your instincts. If something doesn't feel right, it probably isn't.

25. Avoid the person from then on.

Tragedy

Your Dilemma:

**"A good friend of our son's died in a car accident last week.
How do we help our child find comfort?"**

or

**"Liza saw a tragic fire on TV. A girl her age died in the blaze.
Now Liza's afraid that something bad is going to happen to her, too."**

ACTION TIPS

◆ Provide ways for young people to discuss the event, its effects, and their feelings about it. Examples might include youth involvement in town meetings and small-group discussions at school.

◆ Be there when your children need someone to listen. Give them your full attention. Also, let your adolescents know what your feelings are regarding the event and what you are doing to cope.

◆ Reassure your children that you're doing all you can to keep them safe.

◆ Allow them to participate in activities that lead to healing—such as attending memorial services or assisting victims and their families.

FACT: After the events of September 11, 35 percent of children displayed at least one sign of substantial stress, such as avoiding talking about what happened; having trouble concentrating or sleeping; or becoming irritable, grouchy, and easily upset.

From: Center for the Advancement of Health

Tragic events have always been part of life—violence and disaster have been with us since the beginning of time. But our children are growing up in particularly volatile times, and media coverage of tragedy magnifies the horror as it brings it into our living rooms. We are besieged by disturbing images and shocked by the dangerous world in which we live.

Young people are especially vulnerable to the emotional impact of these traumatic events, but they are also resilient human beings. When a tragedy occurs close to home—whether it's a friend's fatal car accident, a suicide, a school shooting, or a terrorist attack that rocks the world—adolescents need help sorting through the complicated feelings brought on by such events. They also need guidance to find healthy ways to grieve and, ultimately, to carry on.

In the aftermath of a tragedy, adults may find it difficult enough to deal with our own feelings of grief, anger, helplessness, and fear. At such times, reaching out to the young people in our lives is certainly challenging, especially if the adolescent tends to shrug off our help. Yet reaching out—again and again—is precisely the response that will model for them the life-affirming and healing power of human connection.

The developmental assets are positive qualities, experiences, and skills that children need to grow up healthy and responsible. Parents, grandparents, stepparents, or any other guardian of a child can use these assets as a framework to help them think through the new experiences they're encountering with their children. The following assets and larger asset categories—Support, Positive Family Communication, Safety, and Service to Others—may help focus your efforts to nurture your children in times of tragedy.

ASSET TYPE	ASSET NAME	ASSET DESCRIPTION
Support	Asset #1 Family Support Asset #2 Positive Family Communication Asset #3 Other Adult Relationships Asset #4 Caring Neighborhood Asset #5 Caring School Climate Asset #6 Parent Involvement in Schooling	Young people need to experience support, care, and love from families and many others. They need organizations and institutions that provide positive, supportive environments.
Support	Positive Family Communication	Young people turn to their parents for advice and support. They have frequent, in-depth conversations with each other on a variety of topics. Parents are approachable and available when their children want to talk.
Empowerment	Safety	Young people feel safe at home, at school, and in their neighborhood.
Empowerment	Service to Others	Young people serve in the community one or more hours per week.

SUPPORT

Sharing feelings about a tragic experience is one powerful means of healing. (Keep in mind, however, that some people prefer to deal with their feelings more privately.) **It is important for adults to provide situations in which young people can discuss the event, its implications, and their feelings about it.** Possibilities for involving youth in dialogue about the tragedy include:

- Informal conversations with parents, teachers, and adult friends;

- Youth forums led by your place of worship;

- Youth involvement in town meetings or other events in the wider community;

- Creative projects, such as writing or other artistic activities, which encourage exploration of the topic;

- Small-group discussions at school;

- Formal counseling if this seems appropriate; and/or

- Meeting with a local debriefing response team to assist staff, students, and parents in addressing their reactions to the aftermath of the event.

POSITIVE FAMILY COMMUNICATION

One of the best things adults can do when young people are expressing strong feelings is simply to listen. Resist the temptation to minimize their pain or loss, disagree with them, or try to cheer them up. **Simply being heard and acknowledged can be a great relief.**

It can be helpful for young people to hear their parents and other adults talk about their own emotional responses to the situation. It's also important for them to see the ways in which you're finding support yourself, such as talking with friends or attending community events. Seeing that you have strong and sometimes confused feelings can help provide context for their own feelings. But make it clear that you are actively working at healing. Hearing you describe the ways you're taking care of your own needs during the crisis—whether giving service to others, talking, praying—demonstrates that a healthy emotional response is possible. Young people are then less likely to feel responsibility to take care of you as well as themselves.

SAFETY

Feeling safe is a prerequisite to action and recovery. In times of crisis, everyone needs reassurance. If there is an immediate threat to their security, **young people need to know that the adults are doing everything possible to ensure their safety.** Fear is normal under such circumstances and should be a topic of continuing discussion, but restoring an atmosphere of safety should be a priority.

SERVICE TO OTHERS

Once young people feel safe, **translating feelings into action will help empower them and relieve the sense of helplessness that often accompanies loss.** Doing something about the situation can be a tremendous relief. Young people can be encouraged to:

- Start a neighborhood fund drive to raise money for victims of the tragedy or for a memorial fund;

- Prepare cards or write letters to families of victims;

- Participate in a memorial service or create a monument for the victims;

- Offer practical assistance, such as grocery shopping or lawn care, to victims' families if appropriate;

- Volunteer at an established relief organization, such as the Red Cross;

- Write letters to legislators expressing their concerns;

- Circulate a petition calling for appropriate action; and/or

- Organize a community or peer-group event to discuss other ways to help.

A LIGHT TOWARD THE FUTURE

Adolescents often work hard at appearing self-sufficient and in control. When tragedy strikes, however, some of this veneer can be stripped away, leaving only the distressing feelings of vulnerability that lie beneath. Young people need to know these feelings are not only normal and healthy, but also a deep expression of our shared humanity.

By engaging young people in the difficult task of coming to terms with tragedy, we can guide them through the crisis and help them heal. As we offer them our love, respect, and patience, and as we demonstrate our own courage, vulnerability, generosity, and resilience, we give them what they need to become kind, dedicated, spirited human beings—the kind of people our world needs.

When Tragedy Occurs—Questions for Discussion

A tragic event calls on all of us to deepen our compassion and empathy for other human beings. For youth, such an event can provide an opportunity for moral development. Grappling with the implications and consequences of a tragedy can strengthen young people's understanding of their place in the world, affirm the importance of treating others with kindness and respect, and teach them to celebrate each moment of life. It can help them open their hearts to the world.

When a tragedy occurs, discussing some of the following questions with adolescents may be useful:

- What is the most memorable part of the situation to you?

- What is the worst part of the event?

- What sort of physical reactions did you have after experiencing or first hearing about the situation?

- How have you been able to get through these tough times?

- Can you think of anyone in your school, neighborhood, or community who is suffering? Do other people's actions contribute to their suffering?

- Do you think everyone suffers? Can you think of anyone who doesn't?

- Are you aware of pain or sorrow in your own life? How does a tragic event make us feel about our own suffering? Does it mean our own suffering doesn't matter?

- Do you think we have a responsibility to help others who are in pain if we can?

- Does the suffering of people we don't know have anything to do with us? Should we care?

Helpful Guides for Parents and Their Adolescents

The Asset Approach
(A great handout for sharing the power of assets with others.) Published by Search Institute

An Asset Builder's Guide to Youth and Money by Jolene L. Roehlkepartain. Published by Search Institute

Assets Happening Here
(Video for teens by teens.) Produced by Noodlehead Network

Ideas for Parents
(Newsletter master set.) Published by Search Institute

In Good Company: Tools to Help Youth and Adults Talk by Franklin W. Nelson, D. Min. Published by Search Institute

Parenting with a Purpose: A Positive Approach for Raising Confident, Caring Youth by Dean Feldmeyer and Eugene C. Roehlkepartain. Published by Search Institute

Step by Step: A Young Person's Guide to Positive Community Change by The Mosaic Youth Center Board members with Jennifer Griffin-Wiesner. Published by Search Institute

Stopping at Every Lemonade Stand: How to Create a Culture that Cares for Kids by James Volbracht. Published by Penguin Books

Succeed Every Day: Daily Readings for Teens by Pamela Espeland. Published by Free Spirit Publishing

Tag, You're It!: 50 Easy Ways to Connect with Young People by Kathleen Kimball-Baker. Published by Search Institute

What Kids Need to Succeed: Proven, Practical Ways to Raise Good Kids by Peter L. Benson, Ph.D., Judy Galbraith, M.A., and Pamela Espeland. Published by Free Spirit Publishing (Spanish version available)

What Teens Need to Succeed: Proven, Practical Ways to Shape Your Own Future by Peter L. Benson, Ph.D., Judy Galbraith, M.A., and Pamela Espeland. Published by Free Spirit Publishing

You can find these resources and more at the Search Institute Web site—www.search-institute.org

Handouts by Asset Category and Asset

Each article in this book addresses numerous assets and asset categories.
The following chart is organized by the assets discussed in each of them.

ASSET CATEGORY AND ASSET	ARTICLE
E X T E R N A L A S S E T S	
Support	The Internet Money Separation or Divorce Single Parenting Substance Abuse Tragedy
Family support	Getting Along: Parents and Adolescents Getting Along: Brothers and Sisters Chores Food Graduation and Beyond Bullying/Being Bullied School Violence Friends Dating Sexuality Self-Acceptance Depression Body Image Separation or Divorce
Positive family communication	Getting Along: Parents and Adolescents Getting Along: Brothers and Sisters TV The Internet Chores Curfew Food Graduation and Beyond Bullying/Being Bullied School Violence Other Caring, Responsible Adults Dating Sexuality Stress Management Self-Acceptance Anger Management Depression Jobs Outside the Home Money

ASSET CATEGORY AND ASSET	ARTICLE
(Positive family communication cont.)	Appearance Body Image Separation or Divorce Race and Ethnicity Substance Abuse Tragedy
Other adult relationships	Getting Along: Parents and Adolescents School Violence Depression Body Image Separation or Divorce Substance Abuse
Caring neighborhood	Other Caring, Responsible Adults
Caring school climate	Bullying/Being Bullied School Violence Other Caring, Responsible Adults Depression Body Image
Parent involvement in schooling	School Violence
Empowerment	Chores
Community values youth	Sexuality Self-Acceptance
Youth as resources	Single Parenting
Service to others	Body Image Tragedy
Safety	The Internet Bullying/Being Bullied School Violence Other Caring, Responsible Adults Dating Appearance Tragedy

ASSET CATEGORY AND ASSET	ARTICLE
Boundaries and Expectations	
Family boundaries	Getting Along: Parents and Adolescents Getting Along: Brothers and Sisters TV The Internet Chores Curfew Dating Sexuality Anger Management Appearance Substance Abuse
School boundaries	
Neighborhood boundaries	
Adult role models	TV Curfew Graduation and Beyond School Violence Friends Stress Management Anger Management Money
Positive peer influence	Friends Dating Self-Acceptance Body Image Substance Abuse
High expectations	Getting Along: Parents and Adolescents School and Homework Graduation and Beyond Sexuality Substance Abuse
Constructive Use of Time	The Internet School Violence Dating Jobs Outside the Home
Creative activities	TV Substance Abuse

ASSET CATEGORY AND ASSET	ARTICLE
Youth programs	TV Other Caring, Responsible Adults
Religious community	Other Caring, Responsible Adults
Time at home	

INTERNAL ASSETS

Commitment to Learning	Food School and Homework Money
Achievement motivation	Graduation and Beyond
School engagement	School and Homework
Homework	School and Homework
Bonding to school	School and Homework School Violence
Reading for pleasure	TV School and Homework
Positive Values	
Caring	Bullying/Being Bullied
Equality and social justice	Race and Ethnicity
Integrity	Race and Ethnicity
Honesty	The Internet Bullying/Being Bullied
Responsibility	Chores Curfew Graduation and Beyond Bullying/Being Bullied Jobs Outside the Home